Thomas Aquinas

Treatise on Law

Thomas Aquinas

Treatise on Law

Translated, with Introduction, Notes, and Glossary, by
RICHARD J. REGAN

Hackett Publishing Company, Inc.
Indianapolis/Cambridge

22 21 20 19 18   4 5 6 7 8

For further information, please address:

Hackett Publishing Company, Inc.
P.O. Box 44937
Indianapolis, IN 46244–0937

www.hackettpublishing.com

Cover design by Listenberger Design & Associates

Library of Congress Cataloging-in-Publication Data
Thomas, Aquinas, Saint, 1225?–1274.
    [Summa theologica. English. Selections]
    Treatise on Law / Thomas Aquinas ; translated, with introduction, notes,
and glossary, by Richard J. Regan.
        p.   cm.
    Includes bibliographical references and index.
    ISBN 0-87220-549-5 (cloth)—ISBN 0-87220-548-7 (paper)
    1. Natural law.   2. Law—Philosophy.   I. Regan, Richard J.   II. Title
K447.T45 S85213 2000
340'.1—dc21   00-039539

CONTENTS

PREFACE

The writings of Thomas Aquinas on morals and law deserve wide circulation for a host of reasons. No student of moral and legal thought can be considered well grounded in the Western tradition if the contribution of the Middle Ages to that tradition is ignored. All too often, courses in moral and legal philosophy skip rapidly from the ancients to the moderns with little comment on the medieval period. Thomas Aquinas, of course, is not the only or even, perhaps, the characteristic theorist of that era in the Christian West. But his ideas ought to be more familiar than those of others because we inherit from him an important notion of natural law. A full, inexpensive translation of Aquinas's treatise on law in the *Summa Theologica* will enable the student to judge firsthand the contribution of that inheritance. This edition omits only sections of the treatise that deal with particulars of the Old and New Laws. To assist the reader, I have provided a glossary of key terms and a select bibliography.

Translators should be faithful to the text and also should express the meaning of the text in felicitous English. The two objectives are often difficult to reconcile. Fidelity to the text has been my priority, but I am confident that the reader will find the translation clear and idiomatic. The translation of some key words often varies with the context and/or involves interpretation. For example, I have variously translated "ratio," the generic Latin word for "reason," as "argument," "aspect," "nature," "plan," "reason," or "reasoning," as appropriate in different contexts. Notes in several places indicate why I chose a particular English word as appropriate.

I wish to thank Patrick Corrigan (St. Anselm's College) and Paul Seaton (Fordham University) for their helpful suggestions. Thanks are also due to William P. Baumgarth, Francis P. Canavan, W. Norris Clarke, Brian Davies, and Louis B. Pascoe (all of Fordham University) for their advice.

Note on the Text

The translation is from the 1952 Marietti recension of the Leonine text. In citing books of the Bible, I have followed the Revised Standard Version. I have followed the Hebrew numbering of the Psalms. (The reader should note that the Psalm verse numbers in English translations are frequently one lower than the Hebrew numbers.) I have translated Thomas Aquinas's biblical quotations as he phrases them, not as they appear in the Vulgate. I have cited Plato according to the Stephanus divisions, and Aristotle according to the Bekker divisions. For patristic citations or quotations, I have referred the reader to the Migne edition.

Richard J. Regan
Bronx, New York

BIBLICAL ABBREVIATIONS

Cor.	Corinthians
Dt.	Deuteronomy
Ex.	Exodus
Gal.	Galatians
Gen.	Genesis
Heb.	Hebrews
Hos.	Hosea
Is.	Isaiah
Jgs.	Judges
Jn.	John
Kgs.	Kings
Lev.	Leviticus
Lk.	Luke
Mc.	Maccabees
Mt.	Matthew
Num.	Numbers
Pet.	Peter
Prov.	Proverbs
Ps.	Psalms
Rom.	Romans
Sam.	Samuel
Sir.	Sirach
Tim.	Timothy
Wis.	Wisdom

OTHER ABBREVIATIONS

A., AA.	Article, Articles
ad	response to objection
c.	chapter
dist.	distinction
Lat.	Latin
n.	number
obj.	objection
PG	J. P. Migne, *Patrologia Graeca*
PL	J. P. Migne, *Patrologia Latina*
Q., QQ.	Question, Questions
ST	Thomas Aquinas, *Summa Theologica*
v.	verse

INTRODUCTION

There are many diverse, and widely diverse, contemporary views about ethics and moral judgments. This pluralism of views seems to make the quest for certainty a formidable task for specialists and ordinary citizens alike. Indeed, some contemporary views go so far as to reduce moral judgments to expressions of emotional likes and dislikes. But at least some moral judgments purport to express opinions about what we or others *should* do or not do, not merely about what we like or dislike. Accordingly, it seems appropriate to ask whether there be objective, that is, reasonable, grounds to justify the judgments as moral imperatives.

As the title and the prologue make clear, the *Summa Theologica* is expressly theological. But it is also a synthesis of Aristotelian philosophy and Christian revelation. Regarding ethics and law, the *Summa* integrates Aristotle's philosophy of the natural good into the biblical tradition of divine law. This introduction cannot do justice to the complexity of Aristotle's ethical views or the biblical moral tradition, but each can be summarily outlined.

The Aristotelian Component

For Aristotle, every kind of thing is ordained for a specific goal, and human beings are ordained for a specifically human good. This human good, which results in the condition of well-being or happiness, consists of activities of reason itself and of other activities according to the judgments of right reason. Activities of reason itself involve intellectual virtues, which concern understanding, scientific knowledge, and theoretical wisdom (knowledge of the ultimate causes of things). Other human activities involve moral virtues, which characteristically dispose human beings toward good action, and the practical intellectual virtue of moral reasoning, the virtue of practical wisdom or prudence, determines the appropriateness of means to achieve moral virtue.

Aristotle's epistemology is realist: external reality is the measure of consciousness, and consciousness the window on external reality. Human beings through their sense cognition perceive an extramental material world and the things in it, and human beings through their intellectual cognition understand the essential structure or nature of different kinds of material things, including their own. And human beings through their intellectual activity also know themselves as the source of their internal activities and external actions.

We tend to identify intellectual activity with the process of reasoning, of drawing inferences from observed facts and general principles. This reasoning can be theoretical or practical. In empirical sciences, scientists, among other things, form theories to explain observed events, deduce consequences from the theory that can be observed, and then test to see whether the deduced consequences occur. If the consequences do occur, the theory is supported but not conclusively verified; if the consequences do not occur, the theory is demonstratively false. In mathematics, mathematicians employ pure deduction to draw conclusions from postulated premises. In everyday affairs, human beings employ both inductive and deductive reasoning to reach conclusions about everything from the feature of tomorrow's weather to the best route to use during rush-hour traffic.

But Aristotle identified another intellectual activity, and this is the activity with which we are principally concerned here: the activity by which we understand the essential structure or nature of things. In the case of human beings themselves, we are capable of understanding that we engage in intellectual activities not only in reasoning from premises but also and chiefly in understanding the nature and end of things. Human understanding is at the heart of Aristotle's philosophy generally and of his ethical theory specifically.

The central theme of Aristotle's metaphysics is that the nature of things determines their type of activity and, conversely, that their specific type of activity indicates the things' nature. Plants, horses, and human beings have different ends and act in specifically different ways to achieve their ends. In Aristotle's view, the essence or nature of things, their specific ends, and the ordination of activities to ends are intelligible to human beings.

Aristotle recognizes rationality in all its dimensions, that is, both activities of reason itself (intellectual virtue) and activities in accord with right reason (moral virtue), as the characteristic that specifically distinguishes the activity of human beings from that of other animals. Human beings, of course, have animal appetites that they act to satisfy: they eat to satisfy hunger, they seek to avoid pain, and they engage in sexual activity. But as long as they act consciously, the animal activities are not merely animal but are *also* subject to judgments of reason. That is to say, human beings have to make judgments about the relation of animal activities to the human end: they have to decide when and how much is humanly proper for them to eat, how to avoid and alleviate pain in humanly proper ways, and when and with whom it is humanly proper for them to have sex. They perceive food and sex as good for them, but they also, on reflection, understand that food and sex are not always good for them as individual human beings and as members of human society. And so human beings are presented with choices in their conscious activities. Human beings can understand their essential constitution and much about the world in terms of cause and effect (for example, that eating or drinking too much will make them sick, that indiscriminate sex will cause harm to others). And human beings by their free acts determine how they are to live in the world. Moreover, Aristotle insisted that human intelligence and freedom open human beings to the friendship and love of other human beings.

Human well-being consists of activities of reason itself, intellectually virtuous activities; and external activities according to the judgments of right reason, morally virtuous activities. If human beings so act, they achieve their human well-being, that is, happiness. Aristotle's concept of moral obligation is hypothetical: if human beings wish to achieve their specific goal of human well-being, they should engage in activities of reason and in external activities according to right reason. Human beings cannot choose any ultimate good except the one specified by their nature, but they are free to choose means conducive to, or destructive of, achievement of their ultimate good. Virtue makes human beings happy and fulfilled, but vice makes them unhappy and unfulfilled.

Aristotle situated the quest for virtue quintessentially within a structured society with other human beings. For Aristotle and ancient Greeks generally, only those who were more than human (pure spirits) or less than human (brute animals) could be fulfilled apart from the *polis* (the Greek city-state), and Aristotle accordingly devoted an entire work, the *Politics,* to the right ordering of the *polis,* which would develop intellectually and morally virtuous citizens. Human beings are by their nature inclined to live in community with other human beings, and human reason should recognize that they should do so to be happy.

The first level of human society is the family. Because human beings by their nature incline to mate and procreate, they form nuclear families, and nuclear families form extended families of blood relatives and in-laws. Out of these extended families come clans and tribes. But neither families nor small groups of families can adequately provide for their well-being, for their physical security, or for their economic sufficiency. Moreover and especially, they cannot adequately provide a broad base for the development of intellectual and moral virtue or for the cultivation of personal friendships. Only a larger, politically organized society can adequately do so.

The Biblical Component

The biblical moral perspective on the behavior expected of the covenanted people of Israel was quite different from that of Aristotle on the behavior requisite for human well-being. A personal and provident God created the universe and the human beings who inhabit it, and his covenant with Israel imposed a code of behavior on the people. What Yahweh commanded was obligatory, and what Yahweh prohibited was sinful. Gen. 2:17 describes God as explicitly commanding Adam and Eve not to eat the fruit of the tree of knowledge of good and evil; consequently, they are punished for disobeying that command. Later, the covenant between God and the Israelites, along with being a loving relationship, brought with it the obligations of the Torah and the Levitical Law.

The Gospels represent the Pharisees and other Jewish leaders at the time of Jesus as more preoccupied with external observance of the Law than with interior dispositions in the cultivation of religious virtue. The Gospels represent Jesus as critical of this preoccupation with ritual observance but not as abrogating the claims of the Law to obedience.

In the course of evangelizing the Gentiles, St. Paul absolved them from any obligation to observe external rituals of the Law, but he held them bound to observe the Law's essentials. In the celebrated passage of Rom. 2:14–16, Paul claims that the Gentiles have essentials of the Law written in their hearts, that they carry out these precepts by reason of their nature (*physei*), and that their consciences will condemn them on the day of judgment if they fail to do so. The essential moral demands of the Law on the people of Israel, as expressed in the Ten Commandments, are seen as God's moral demands on all human beings by the constitution of human nature itself.

The Synthesis

Thomas Aquinas is in basic agreement with Aristotle that human happiness consists of activities of the soul, namely, theoretical intellectual activities and, in this life, practical intellectual activities. But when Aquinas comes to specify the object of human happiness, he decisively parts company with Aristotle; the object of human happiness, says Aquinas, is the intellectual, albeit not comprehensive, intuition of God's essence in itself, the fullness of being that will completely satisfy the desire of human beings to know and understand. Aquinas argues that human beings will not be perfectly happy as long as there remains something more for them to know, that they are constituted by nature to seek to know God, and that they in this life cannot know what God is in himself.

Aristotle was satisfied with the limited, albeit daunting, goal of theoretical wisdom as the most important ingredient of human happiness. Aquinas agrees with Aristotle that theoretical wisdom is a major ingredient of happiness in this life, and that human beings, in order to be happy in this life, need a suitable body, external goods, and the company of friends. But Aquinas insists that the happiness attainable in this life is incomplete and imperfect, a pale reflection of the perfect happiness of beholding God's essence, and that no material or created spiritual thing, including human friendship, is essential to such perfect happiness.

Both Aristotle and Aquinas recognize that human happiness in this life also requires right reason to direct external action and govern internal emotions, as well as a rightly ordered will regarding the requisite ends of human actions and emotions. But Aquinas goes beyond Aristotle to maintain that rectitude of the will is necessary for happiness because willing requisite ends necessarily entails loving as good whatever God loves. For Aquinas, there is no complete rectitude of will without conformity to God's will and his commands. Revelation and reason communicate God's commands, and so human beings should conform their will to the divine commands of both. Although it may be true, as Aquinas thought and as probably most Christians then and now think, that there can be no real conflict between right reason and Christian duty, there remain questions about whether particular moral judgments of reason are right, whether Christian faith imposes particular religious duties, and how to reconcile apparent conflicts.

The goodness of the will depends exclusively on the will's object, and so it depends on reason, which presents the object to the will as in accord or discord with reason. Since the light of human reason participates in the eternal law, the goodness or malice of the will depends even more on that law. Every will acting contrary to reason, even erroneous reason, is evil, but some acts of the will in accord with erroneous reason may be evil, since human beings may be directly or indirectly (through vincible ignorance) responsible for the fact that their reason judges erroneously.

The most striking contrast between Aquinas's treatment of human acts and Aristotle's is the attention Aquinas pays to the moral goodness and malice of individual human acts. Aristotle was largely concerned about the moral character of human acts in connection with the development of moral virtue, that is, with the consequences of morally good and bad acts for acquiring morally good or bad habits. But Aquinas, although similarly concerned about that result of human acts, is also and primarily concerned about the moral character of individual human acts for gaining heavenly blessedness or incurring eternal damnation. That is to say, he is concerned about the moral character of human acts not only in relation to dictates of right reason and to the acquisition of virtue in this life, but also and primarily in relation to dictates of God's law and to the acquisition of the beatific vision in the next life.

For Aristotle, a virtuous life constitutes its own reward and a vicious life constitutes its own punishment. For Aquinas, a virtuous life in this world does not confer complete happiness on human beings, and a vicious life does not sufficiently punish human beings with unhappiness. Moreover, not only are morally bad acts bad for their perpetrators, in Aquinas's view, but they are also and primarily offenses against God and for that very reason are justly punished by him. Accordingly, the morality of every human act involving serious matter is of supreme importance for human beings. For example, murder is not only contrary to the humanity of the murderer and an offense against the victim but also a serious offense against God, who justly inflicts the punishment of hell on unrepentant murderers. Conversely, just acts are not only acts that are just to others and virtuous but also acts that God's grace can render salvific, that is, worthy of heavenly reward.

Thomas Aquinas holds that some external acts are intrinsically evil, since the acts frustrate the intrinsic ends of the acts. For example, he argues that lying is always wrong because it frustrates the intrinsic purpose of communicative speech (ST II–II, Q. 110, A. 1). Similarly, he argues that some sexual behavior is always wrong because it is contrary to the intrinsic purpose of sex (ST II–II, Q. 154, especially A. 11). Such a position rests on the unarticulated premise that no larger purpose, however good, can render the evil acts morally good, and the position differs at least from the emphasis of Aristotle.

In his treatment of moral virtues, Aquinas follows Aristotle in many respects. As with Aristotle, the key virtue in moral matters is intellectual. Practical wisdom, that is, practical reason, directs the moral virtues by prescribing their ends (for example, to be just, moderate, courageous) and by choosing the means to achieve those ends. And in the cultivation and mastery of emotions, Aquinas echoes Aristotle on the necessity of habituation. But Aquinas does not rest there. To live a consistently virtuous life, human beings after the fall of Adam need added help. And so, to strengthen their radically weakened natural power, God infuses supernatural moral virtues and the theological virtue of charity, which informs every moral virtue, whether naturally acquired or supernaturally infused, in those he justifies.

Neither Aristotle nor Aquinas is optimistic about the possibility or likelihood of most human beings' living a virtuous life. Natural aptitude, of course, will decidedly limit the possibility of most persons in acquiring intellectual virtues, and the dominance of inordinate desires will limit the possibility of most persons, left to themselves, in acquiring moral virtues.

But both Aristotle and Aquinas think that a rightly organized community could considerably rectify the moral situation, although moral evil and its social consequences can never be eliminated. Both Aristotle and Aquinas look to enlightened political leaders, that is, to those with the virtue of a specific practical wisdom, political prudence, to guide the community by framing laws that encourage virtue and discourage vice. Political prudence, as practical reason, should do so only in reasonable ways, sometimes punishing vice, sometimes rewarding virtue, sometimes refraining from doing either. Coercion is appropriate only to repress vices harmful to society, and it is most appropriate to repress the vices most harmful to society (for example, murder, robbery).

Thomas Aquinas looks primarily to the church to inculcate moral virtue in the faithful. The church will accomplish this, in part, by promising heavenly blessedness to the virtuous and by threatening sinners with the punishment of hell. But if both the church and the state are assigned authoritative roles in the sphere of moral virtue, conflict is likely and almost inevitable unless the respective roles are clearly distinguished. Although Aquinas did distinguish the two roles, he subordinated the temporal power of the state to the spiritual power of the church in cases of conflict. However theoretically untenable this subordination of the temporal power of the state to the spiritual power of the church, it is noteworthy how much Aquinas's vision of the role of religion in organized society differs from that of Aristotle. For Aristotle and the Greeks generally, religion was a necessary part of civic life that required of citizens only ritual observance. For Aquinas, the Christian religion calls the faithful to a comprehensive way of life, and the Christian church inculcates a comprehensive moral code of conduct.

God's act of creation is the foundation of Aquinas's theory of moral obligation as legally obligatory. By that very act, God ordains created things for their specific goals, and specific goals for an architechtonic goal, and he manifests his ordinance in the natures that he creates. Aquinas can properly refer to God's act of creation as law because God ordains the activities of creatures, and as eternal because his act is identical with himself.

Irrational creatures have no freedom regarding their actions, and human beings have no choice regarding their specific goal or the rectitude of means to that goal. However, human beings are free to act or not to act in ways conducive to their specific goal, and so human beings participate rationally and freely in the eternal law. When human beings act in accord with their nature, they share with their reason and will in God's plan for themselves as individuals and as a community. And so Aquinas can properly refer to this human participation in the eternal law as natural law. Contrary to the Kantian critique of natural-law theory, Aquinas, by assigning a participatory role to human beings in legislating eternal law for and to themselves, recognizes the necessity of personal autonomy for authentic moral decisions.

Thomas Aquinas was a Christian theologian. He considered creation, and so natural law, as one aspect of God's salvific plan for humankind. Whereas Aristotle rested content with human goodness in a self-sufficient *polis,* Aquinas was concerned as well with Christian holiness and with obedience to God's commands explicit or implicit in his creative act and salvific will. In this regard, the natural law has a supernatural dimension: observance of the natural law can be a grace-enriched act, and failure to observe the natural law is a sinful act. In Aquinas's view, divine revelation plays a supportive role in recognizing demands of the natural law, and divine grace an indispensable role in its consistent and substantial observance. Moreover, love of God is the guiding source of the morally virtuous activity of the Christian faithful.

For both Aristotle and Aquinas, human beings need to form a body politic in order to promote their proper human development, that is, to develop themselves intellectually and morally as well as materially. But Aquinas goes further: he links human law essentially to natural law. Human law is either a conclusion based on the natural law (for example, do not steal) or a further determination of natural law (for example, drive on the right side of the road). This linkage is absolutely essential if human law is to qualify as law at all, that is, to be morally obligatory. And human law, if it departs from the natural law in any way, is no law at all, that is, not morally obligatory. Thomas Aquinas, however, admits that citizens may be morally obliged to obey some unjust laws, if those laws are not contrary to divine law, in order to preserve the common good, that is, to avoid civil unrest and the breakdown of law (ST I–II, Q. 96, A. 4).

Other Moral and Legal Theories

There are alternate ways of systematizing moral and legal theory. We cannot do justice to these, but we can summarily indicate several principal theories. One alternative relies exclusively on divine revelation and illumination. The Reformers of the sixteenth century (for example, Martin Luther and John Calvin) adopted this position, as do some Protestant traditions today. The Reformers thought that the fall of Adam from original grace was total, so that human nature became radically depraved, and that all human acts as a result are inherently sinful, even the acts of the just. In the Reformers' view, human reason with the fall of Adam became too enfeebled to recognize moral norms without the aid of divine revelation, and the human will too debased to act in unqualifiedly virtuous ways. Prescinding from the theological aspects of this position, one may ask whether the traditional Protestant view of the condition of sinful human beings needs to exclude the concept of natural law entirely. One may also ask how human beings, without using reason, can form moral judgments about the many particular questions on which the Bible is silent or unspecific.

Another theory is that of utilitariansim, of which there are many versions, even some Christian versions (for example, situation ethics and, to a lesser extent, proportionalism). The versions all share a basic conviction that the morality of human action should be judged by whether the action results in the greatest good of the greatest number, however that principle is interpreted. This principle requires a rigorous philosophical analysis, but it will suffice here to ask a fundamental question: can any beneficial results, of whatever kind or magnitude, and for however many human beings, *justify* the direct killing of even one *innocent* human being?

Immanuel Kant and legal positivists radically divorce the moral and juridical orders. For them, morals exclusively concern the internal, private life of the individual, and positive law exclusively concerns the external, public life of the human beings in society. However, individuals live in the external world of human interaction, and morally conscious individuals assume that their external activity or inactivity has consequences for their moral integrity. Again, without prejudice to a rigorous philosophical analysis, one may ask why, if we adopt this position, we should condemn those who carried out or failed to resist the formally legal commands of German officials under the Nazi regime.

We should also note that many of the American Founding Fathers held a theory of natural right and natural law. Echoing John Locke, the Declaration of Independence asserted it to be self-evident "that all men are created equal, that they are endowed by their creator with certain unalienable rights" and that governments are instituted to secure those rights. Since human beings have natural rights, that is, rights from nature, the law of nature and nature's God obliges human beings to respect the rights of others. Although this view of natural law is more individual and limited than Aquinas's, the theory of Locke and the Founding Fathers nonetheless has much in common with Thomist and English common-law traditions.

The Structure and Method of the *Summa Theologica*

The *Summa* is divided into three parts. In the first part, Thomas Aquinas considers God and our predications about him, creation, angels, the constitution of human beings, and Adam's condition before the fall. The second part, itself divided into two parts, deals with the ultimate end of human beings, the nature of specifically human acts, sin, law, and the virtues. The third part deals with how Christ redeemed and saved the human race and how the sacraments communicate the fruits of Christ's mediation. The *Summa* thus progresses cyclically: human beings come from God and, despite Adam's fall, are destined to return to God if they freely cooperate with the graces won by Christ and communicated by the sacraments.

The treatise on law is from the first part of the second part of the *Summa* and deals with Aquinas's views on the objective moral aspect of human decision making. He poses a series of questions related to this topic, and the questions are divided into articles raising specific points of inquiry. Each article poses a problem in the form of a question. The article begins with objections to the position that Aquinas will adopt. Each objection cites at least one scriptural, patristic, theological, philosophical, or popular statement. He then declares his contrary position, typically citing a scriptural, patristic, or philosophical text in support. Next, Aquinas elaborates one or more arguments in favor of his position. Lastly, he answers each objection in turn. Although many of the objections are superficial or are plays on words, others provide the opportunity for him to make clarifications or distinctions that he deems important.

Why do the articles have this formal structure? The short answer lies in the fact that the *Summa* reflects, albeit with significant modifications, academic conventions of the University of Paris and of other medieval universities. Faculty masters or student degree-candidates would at appointed times defend theses against all comers, and the format resembled that of a modern debate. The first step in the process was to recapitulate an opponent's position in such a way that the opponent could agree that his position was correctly stated and interpreted. Only then would the master or student defend his own position.

The longer explanation of the formal structure of the articles in the *Summa* is that the medieval thesis-defense format invited audience participation in a way similar to that of a Platonic dialogue. As Plato implicitly invites readers of the dialogues to become intellectually involved in the exchange of ideas between Socrates and his interlocutors, so Aquinas and other medieval masters explicitly invited their audience—and implicitly continue to invite readers—to become intellectually involved in resolving the questions posed. The objections in the medieval format thus take on the role of Socrates' interlocutors in the Platonic dialogues.

Unlike the Socrates represented in the dialogues, however, Thomas Aquinas and other medieval masters clearly enunciated their own positions and directly distinguished the terms involved in the discussions. Where

Plato progressively raised a series of questions to indicate the presuppositions of Socrates' interlocutors, as well as the need to go beyond conventional understanding of the world and human experience, Aquinas gives explicit answers to clearly framed questions. In this respect, Aquinas has more in common with modern academic conventions than Plato has, however much both seek to involve their respective audiences.

The questions that Aquinas raised about the objective moral dimension of human activity may need to be reformulated or nuanced. The answers he gave may need to be modified or rejected. New questions may be pertinent. But the topics and his many insights merit careful consideration.

WORKS CITED BY AQUINAS

Albert the Great, St.
Commentary on the Sentences

Ambrose, St.
On Paradise

Aristotle
Categories
Ethics (Nicomachean)
Metaphysics
Physics
Politics
Rhetoric

Augustine, St.
Against Adimantus, Disciple of Mani
On Catechizing the Uneducated
The City of God
Confessions
Eighty-Three Questions
Against Faustus
On Free Choice
On Heresies
Letters
On the Marital Good
On the Spirit and the Letter of the Law
On the Trinity
On True Religion
Against the Two Letters of Pelagius

Basil, St.
On the Six Days of Creation

Boethius
On Groups of Seven

Caesar, Julius
Gallic Wars

Cato, Denis
Concise Opinions and Distichs on Morals

Cicero, Marcus Tullius
On Duties
Rhetoric

Damascene, St. John
On Orthodox Faith

Glossae ordinariae

Gratian
Decretum

Gregory IX, Pope
Decretals

Hilary, St.
On the Trinity

Isidore, St.
Etymologies
Synonyms

Justinian
Code
Digest

Lombard, Peter
Glossae
Sentences

Plato
Timaeus

Authors Cited by Aquinas

Albert the Great, St. (A.D. 1200? –1280)
Ambrose, St. (A.D. 340? –397)
Aristotle, "the Philosopher" (384–327 B.C.)
Augustine, St. (A.D. 354–430)
Basil, St. (A.D. 329? –379)
Boethius (A.D. 480? –524?)
Caesar, Julius (100–44 B.C.)
Cato, Denis (fourth century A.D.)
Cicero, Marcus Tullius (106–43 B.C.)
Damascene, St. John (A.D. 700? –754?)
Gratian (first half of twelfth century A.D.)
Gregory IX, Pope (A.D. 1170? –1241)
Hilary, St. (A.D. 315? –368?)
Isidore, St. (A.D. 560?–636)
Justinian, "the Jurist" (A.D. 483–565)
Lombard, Peter (A.D. 1100? –1160)
Paul, St., "the Apostle" (first century A.D.)
Plato (428? –348/347 B.C.)

ST I–II

QUESTION 90
On the Essence of Law

FIRST ARTICLE
Does Law Belong to Reason?

We thus proceed to the first inquiry. It seems that law does not belong to reason, for the following reasons:

Objection 1. The Apostle in Rom. 7:23 says: "I perceive another law in my bodily members," etc. But nothing belonging to reason belongs to bodily members, since reason does not use bodily organs. Therefore, law does not belong to reason.

Obj. 2. Only power, habits, and acts belong to reason. But law is not the very power of reason. Likewise, law is not a habit of reason, since habits of reason are intellectual virtues, about which I have spoken before.[1] Nor is law an act of reason, since law would cease when the lawmaker ceased to reason (e.g., when he is sleeping). Therefore, law does not belong to reason.

Obj. 3. Law induces those subject to the law to act rightly. But inducing to act rightly belongs in the strict sense to the will, as is evident from what I have said before.[2] Therefore, law belongs to the will rather than to reason, as the Jurist also says: "The pleasure of the ruler has the force of law."[3]

On the contrary, it belongs to law to command and forbid. But to command belongs to reason, as I have maintained before.[4] Therefore, law belongs to reason.

I answer that law is a rule and measure of acts that induces persons to act or refrain from acting. For *law* [Lat.: *lex*] is derived from *binding* [Lat.: *ligare*] because law obliges persons to act. And the rule and measure of human acts is reason, which is the primary source of human acts, as is evident from what I have said before.[5] For it belongs to reason to order us to our end, which is the primary source regarding our prospective action, as the Philosopher says.[6] And the source in any kind of thing is the measure and rule of that kind of thing (e.g., units in numbers and first movements in movements). And so we conclude that law belongs to reason.

Reply Obj. 1. We say that law, since it is a rule or measure, belongs to something in two ways. It belongs in one way as to what measures and

---

[1] I–II, Q. 57. [2] I–II, Q. 9, A. 1. [3] *Digest* I, title 4, law 1. [4] I–II, Q. 17, A. 1. [5] I–II, Q. 1, A. 1, *ad* 3. [6] *Physics* II, 9 (200a22–24).

rules. And law in this way belongs only to reason, since measuring and ruling belong to reason. Law belongs to something in a second way as to what is ruled and measured. And then law applies to everything that a law induces to something, so that we can call every inclination resulting from a law, law by participation, as it were, not essentially. And we in this way call the very inclination of bodily members to concupiscence the law of the bodily members.

Reply Obj. 2. Regarding external acts, we can consider the activity and the product of the activity (e.g., building and the building constructed). Just so, regarding acts of reason, we can consider the very acts of reason (i.e., acts of understanding and reasoning) and the things produced by such acts. And regarding theoretical reason, definitions are indeed the first product. Propositions are the second product. And syllogisms and arguments the third product. And practical reason also uses a kind of syllogism regarding prospective actions, as I have maintained before,[7] and as the Philosopher teaches in the *Ethics*.[8] Therefore, there are things in practical reason that are related to actions as propositions in theoretical reason are related to conclusions. And such universal propositions of practical reason related to actions have the nature[9] of law. And reason indeed sometimes actually contemplates and sometimes only habitually retains these propositions.

Reply Obj. 3. Reason has from the will the power to induce activity, as I have said before,[10] since reason commands means because one wills ends. But an act of reason needs to rule the will regarding the means commanded in order that the willing have the nature of law. And we in this way understand that the will of a ruler has the force of law. Otherwise, the willing of the ruler would be injustice rather than law.

SECOND ARTICLE
Is Law Always Ordained for the Common Good?

We thus proceed to the second inquiry. It seems that law is not ordained for the common good as its end, for the following reasons:

Objection 1. It belongs to law to command and forbid. But precepts are ordained for particular goods. Therefore, the end of law is not always the common good.

---

[7] I–II: Q. 13, A. 3; Q. 76, A. 1; Q. 77, A. 2, *ad* 4.　　[8] *Ethics* VII, 3 (1147a24–31).
[9] "*Ratio*" in this and like contexts (e.g., ST I–II, Q. 94, AA. 2 and 4) signifies the character or essential element of some class of thing, the objective content of the idea of the class. I use the word "nature" here and elsewhere to convey this sense where appropriate.　　[10] I–II, Q. 17, A. 1.

Obj. 2. Law directs the actions of human beings. But human acts regard particulars. Therefore, law is likewise ordained for particular goods.

Obj. 3. Isidore says in his *Etymologies:* "If law is based on reason, everything founded on reason will be law."[11] But both things ordained for the common good and things ordained for private good are based on reason. Therefore, law is ordained both for the common good and for the private good of individuals.

On the contrary, Isidore says in his *Etymologies* that laws are "enacted for no private convenience but for the common benefit of citizens."[12]

I answer that, as I have said,[13] law belongs to the source of human acts, since law is their rule and measure. And as reason is the source of human acts, so also is there in reason itself something that is the source of all other kinds of acts. And so law needs chiefly and especially to belong to this source.

And the first source in practical matters, with which practical reason is concerned, is the ultimate end. But the ultimate end of human life is happiness or blessedness, as I have maintained before.[14] And so law especially needs to regard the ordination to blessedness.

Moreover, law in the strict sense needs to concern ordination to happiness in general, since every part is related to a whole as something imperfect to something perfect. And so also the Philosopher, regarding the cited definition of laws,[15] speaks of both happiness and political community. For he says in the *Ethics* that "we call those laws just that constitute and preserve happiness and its particulars by citizens' sharing in a political community."[16] For the political community is the perfect community, as he says in the *Politics.*[17]

And regarding any kind of thing, the one most such is the source of the others, and we call the others such by their relation to that one. For example, fire, which is hottest, causes heat in composite material substances, which we call hot insofar as they share in fire. And so, since we speak of law in the first place because of its ordination to the common good, every other precept regarding particular acts has the nature of law only because of its ordination to the common good. And so every law is ordained for the common good.

Reply Obj. 1. Precepts signify the application of laws to things regulated by the laws. And the ordination to the common good, which belongs

---

[11]*Etymologies* II, 10 (PL 82:130); V, 3 (PL 82:199).   [12]Ibid. V, 21 (Pl 82:203).
[13]A. 1.   [14] I–II: Q. 2, A. 7; Q. 3, A. 1; Q. 69, A. 1.   [15]In the section *On the contrary.*   [16]*Ethics* V, 1 (1129b17–19).   [17]*Politics* I, 1 (1252a5–7).

to law, can be applied to particular ends. And so there can be precepts even regarding particular matters.

Reply Obj. 2. Actions indeed concern particular matters, but such particulars can be related to the common good by sharing in the final cause, insofar as we call the common good the final cause, not by sharing in a genus or species.

Reply Obj. 3. As theoretical reason firmly establishes nothing except by tracing things back to first indemonstrable principles, so practical reason firmly establishes nothing except by ordering things to our ultimate end, that is, our common good. And what reason so establishes has the nature of law.

THIRD ARTICLE
Is Any Person's Reason Competent to Make Law?

We thus proceed to the third inquiry. It seems that any person's reason is competent to make law, for the following reasons:

Objection 1. The Apostle says in Rom. 2:14 that "when the Gentiles, who do not have the law, by nature do the things the law prescribes, they make law for themselves." But we say the same about everybody. Therefore, anyone can make law for oneself.

Obj. 2. As the Philosopher says in the *Ethics*,[18] "lawmakers aim to induce human beings to virtue." But any human being can lead others to virtue. Therefore, the reason of any human being is competent to make law.

Obj. 3. As the ruler of a political community governs that community, so the head of a household governs his household. But the ruler of a political community can make laws regarding the political community. Therefore, any head of a household can make laws regarding his household.

On the contrary, Isidore says in his *Etymologies*,[19] and the *Decretum*[20] maintains: "Laws are ordinances of the people whereby elders and commoners together prescribe things." Therefore, not every person's reason is competent to make law.

I answer that law in the strict sense primarily and chiefly regards ordaining things for the common good. But ordaining things for the common good belongs either to the whole people[21] or to persons acting in the

---

[18] *Ethics* II, 1 (1103b3–4).   [19] *Etymologies* V, 10 (PL 82:200).   [20] Gratian, *Decretum* I, dist. 2, c. 1.   [21] The Latin word *"multitudo"* literally signifies ordinary people, the many as opposed to the few (usually the rulers). But Thomas Aquinas here uses the word in the same sense as the Latin word *"populus,"* the people as a political unit. The modifying adjective *"whole"* makes this usage clear. Cf. ST I–II, Q. 97, A. 3, *ad* 3, where he uses *"multitudo"* and *"populus"* interchangeably.

name of the whole people. And so lawmaking belongs either to the whole people or to a public personage who has the care of the whole people. For also in all other matters, ordaining things for ends belongs to those to whom the ends belong.

Reply Obj. 1. As I have said before,[22] law belongs both to those who rule, and by participation to those who are ruled. And it is in the latter way that everyone makes law for oneself, as one participates in the ordinations of the ruler. And so also the Apostle adds in v. 15: "And they manifest the law's operation written in their hearts."

Reply Obj. 2. Private persons cannot effectively induce others to virtue. For private persons can only offer advice and have no coercive power if their advice should not be accepted. And law should have coercive power in order to induce others effectively to virtue, as the Philosopher says in the *Ethics*.[23] But the people or a public personage has such coercive power and the right to inflict punishment, as I shall explain later.[24] And so it belongs only to the people or a public personage to make law.

Reply Obj. 3. As human beings are parts of a household, so households are parts of a political community, as the *Politics* says.[25] And so, as the good of a human being is not the ultimate end of that individual but is ordained for the common good, so also the good of a household is ordained for the good of a political community, which is a perfect community. And so those who govern households can indeed make precepts and rules, but such precepts and rules do not have the nature of law in the strict sense.

FOURTH ARTICLE
Is Promulgation an Essential Component of Law?

We thus proceed to the fourth inquiry. It seems that promulgation is not an essential component of law, for the following reasons:

Objection 1. The natural law most has the nature of law. But the natural law does not need to be promulgated. Therefore, promulgation is not an essential component of law.

Obj. 2. Obligation to do or not to do things belongs in the strict sense to law. But both those to whom laws have been promulgated and those to whom laws have not, are obliged to obey laws. Therefore, promulgation is not an essential component of law.

Obj. 3. The obligation to obey laws also extends to the future, since "laws impose obligation regarding future affairs," as the *Code* says.[26] But

---

[22] A. 1, *ad* 1. [23] *Ethics* X, 9 (1180a20). [24] I–II, Q. 92, A. 2, *ad* 3; II–II, Q. 64, A. 3. [25] Aristotle, *Politics* I, 1 (1252a5–7). [26] Justinian, *Code* I, title 14, law 7.

laws are promulgated to those present at their promulgation. Therefore, promulgation is not an essential component of law.

On the contrary, the *Decretum* says that "laws are established when they are promulgated."[27]

I answer that laws are imposed on others as rules and measures, as I have said.[28] But rules and measures are imposed by being applied to those ruled and measured. And so laws, in order to oblige persons, as is proper to law, need to be applied to those who are to be ruled by the laws. But the promulgation leading them to knowledge achieves such application. And so promulgation is necessary for laws to be in force.

And so we can compose the definition of law from the four characteristics I have mentioned: law is an ordination of reason for the common good by one who has the care of the community, and promulgated.

Reply Obj. 1. The natural law is promulgated by God when he implants it in the minds of human beings so that they know it by nature.

Reply Obj. 2. Those to whom a law is not promulgated are obliged to observe it insofar as others make it known to them, or it can become known to them after it has been promulgated.

Reply Obj. 3. The present promulgation of a law reaches into the future through the durability of written words, which in a way are always promulgating it. And so Isidore says in his *Etymologies* that "we derive *law* [Lat.: *lex*] from *reading* [Lat.: *legere*], since law is written."[29]

---

[27] Gratian, *Decretum* I, dist. 4, c. 3. [28] A. 1. [29] *Etymologies* II, 10 (PL 82:130); V, 3 (PL 82:199).

QUESTION 91
On Different Kinds of Law

FIRST ARTICLE
Is There an Eternal Law?

We thus proceed to the first inquiry. It seems that there is no eternal law, for the following reasons:

Objection 1. Every law is imposed on particular persons. But there was no one from eternity on whom law could be imposed, since only God was from eternity. Therefore, no law is eternal.

Obj. 2. Promulgation is an essential component of law. But there could be no promulgation from eternity, since there was no one from eternity to whom a law would be be promulgated. Therefore, no law can be eternal.

Obj. 3. Law signifies the direction to an end. But nothing ordained to an end is eternal, since only the ultimate end is eternal. Therefore, no law is eternal.

On the contrary, Augustine says in his work *On Free Choice:* "No one with intelligence can perceive the law called supreme reason not to be immutable and eternal."[1]

I answer that, as I have said before,[2] law is simply a dictate of practical reason by a ruler who governs a perfect community. But supposing that God's providence rules the world, as I maintained in the First Part,[3] his reason evidently governs the entire community of the universe. And so the plan of governance of the world existing in God as the ruler of the universe has the nature of law. And since God's reason conceives eternally, as Prov. 8:23 says, not temporally, we need to say that such law is eternal.

Reply Obj. 1. Things that do not exist in themselves exist with God insofar as he foreknows and foreordains them, as Rom. 4:17 says: "And he calls nonexisting things into existence." Therefore, the eternal conception of God's law has the nature of an eternal law insofar as he ordains that law for governance of the world he foreknows.

Reply Obj. 2. Word and inscription promulgate law. And God promulgates his eternal law in both ways, since the Word of God and the inscription of the predestined in the Book of Life[4] are eternal. But as

---

[1] *On Free Choice* I, 6, n. 15 (PL 32:1229).   [2] I–II, Q. 90; A. 1, *ad* 2; AA. 3–4.
[3] I, Q. 22, AA. 1, 2.   [4] Cf. I, Q. 24, A. 1.

7

regards the creatures who hear or read God's law, the promulgation cannot be eternal.

Reply Obj. 3. Law signifies actively ordaining things for an end, namely, that law ordain things for an end. And law does not signify being ordained for an end, that is, that law itself be ordained for another end, except incidentally in the case of human rulers, whose end is extrinsic to themselves. And then the rulers' laws also need to be ordained for that extrinsic end. But the end of God's governance is God himself,[5] and his law is indistinguishable from himself. And so the eternal law is not ordained for another end.

SECOND ARTICLE
Is There a Natural Law in Us?

We thus proceed to the second inquiry. It seems that there is no natural law in us, for the following reasons:

Objection 1. The eternal law sufficiently governs human beings. For Augustine says in his work *On Free Choice* that "the eternal law is that whereby it is right that all things be most orderly."[6] But nature does not abound in superfluities, nor is it wanting in necessities. Therefore, there is no natural law for human beings.

Obj. 2. Law ordains human beings to their end regarding their actions, as I have maintained before.[7] But nature does not ordain human actions to their end, as happens in the case of irrational creatures, which act for their ends only by natural appetites. Rather, human beings act for their end by the use of their reason and will. Therefore, there is no natural law for human beings.

Obj. 3. The freer one is, the less one is subject to law. But human beings are freer than all other animals because human beings, unlike other animals, have free choice. Therefore, since other animals are not subject to a natural law, neither are human beings.

On the contrary, a gloss on Rom. 2:14, "When the Gentiles, who do not have the law, do by nature things prescribed by the law," etc., says: "Although they do not have the written law, they have a natural law, whereby each of them understands and is conscious of good and evil."[8]

I answer that, as I have said before,[9] law, since it is a rule or measure, can belong to things in two ways: in one way to those who rule and measure; in a second way to those ruled and measured, since things are ruled or measured

---

[5]Cf. I, Q. 22, A. 1; Q. 103, A. 2.   [6]*On Free Choice* I, 6, n. 15 (PL 32:1229).
[7]I–II, Q. 90, A. 2.   [8]*Glossa ordinaria,* on Rom. 2:14 (PL 114:476); Peter Lombard, *Glossa,* on Rom. 2:14 (PL 191:1345).   [9]I–II, Q. 90, A. 1, *ad* 1.

insofar as they partake of the rule or measure. But the eternal law rules and measures everything subject to God's providence, as is evident from what I have said before.[10] And so everything evidently shares in some way in the eternal law, namely, insofar as all things have inclinations to their own acts and ends from its imprint on them. But the rational creature is subject to God's providence in a more excellent way than other things, since such a creature also shares in God's providence in providing for itself and others. And so it shares in the eternal plan whereby it has its natural inclination to its requisite activity and end. And we call such participation in the eternal law by rational creatures the natural law. And so Ps. 4:6, after saying, "Offer just sacrifices," asks: "Who shows us just things?" and replies: "The light of your countenance, O Lord, has been inscribed on us." The Psalmist thus signifies that the light of natural reason whereby we discern good and evil is simply the imprint of God's light in us. And so it is clear that the natural law is simply rational creatures' participation in the eternal law.

Reply Obj. 1. The argument of this objection would be valid if the natural law were to be something different from the eternal law. But the natural law shares in the eternal law, as I have said.[11]

Reply Obj. 2. Every activity of reason and the will in us is derived from what exists by nature, as I have maintained before,[12] since every process of reasoning is derived from first principles known by nature, and every desire of means is derived from the natural desire of our ultimate end. And so also the natural law needs first to direct our acts to their end.

Reply Obj. 3. Even irrational animals, like rational creatures, share in the eternal law in their own way. But because rational creatures share in the eternal law by using their intellect and reason, we call their participation in the eternal law law in the strict sense, since law belongs to reason, as I have said before.[13] And irrational creatures do not share in the eternal law by the use of reason. And so we can call the latter participation law only by analogy.

THIRD ARTICLE
Are There Human Laws?

We thus proceed to the third inquiry. It seems that there are no human laws, for the following reasons:

Objection. 1. The natural law shares in the eternal law, as I have said.[14] But the eternal law "renders all things most orderly," as Augustine says in his work *On Free Choice*.[15] Therefore, the natural law suffices for ordering all human affairs. Therefore, there is no need for human laws.

---

[10] A. 1.   [11] In the body of the article.   [12] I–II, Q. 10, A. 1.   [13] I–II, Q. 90, A. 1.   [14] A. 2.   [15] *On Free Choice* I, 6, n. 15 (PL 32:1229).

Obj. 2. Law has the nature of a measure, as I have said.[16] But human reason is not the measure of things. Rather, the converse is true, as the *Metaphysics* says.[17] Therefore, human reason can produce no law.

Obj. 3. A measure should be most certain, as the *Metaphysics* says.[18] But dictates of human reason about things to be done are uncertain, as Wis. 9:14 says: "The thoughts of mortal human beings are fraught with fear, and our foresight uncertain." Therefore, human reason cannot produce laws.

On the contrary, Augustine in his work *On Free Choice* posits two kinds of law, one kind eternal, and the other temporal, which he calls human.[19]

I answer that law is a dictate of practical reason, as I have said before.[20] But there are similar processes of practical and theoretical reason, since both proceed from principles to conclusions, as I have maintained before.[21] Therefore, we should say that we advance in theoretical reason from indemonstrable first principles, naturally known, to the conclusions of different sciences, conclusions not implanted in us by nature but discovered by exercising reason. Just so, human reason needs to advance from the precepts of the natural law, as general and indemonstrable first principles, to matters that are to be more particularly regulated. And we call such regulations devised by human reason human laws, provided that the other conditions belonging to the nature of law are observed, as I have said before.[22] And so also Cicero says in his *Rhetoric:* "Human law originally sprang from nature. Then things became customs because of their rational benefit. Then fear and reverence for law validated things that both sprang from nature and were approved by custom."[23]

Reply Obj. 1. Human reason cannot partake of the complete dictates of God's reason but partakes of them in its own way and incompletely. And so regarding theoretical reason, we by our natural participation in God's wisdom know general principles but do not specifically know every truth, as God's wisdom does. Just so regarding practical reason, human beings by nature partake of the eternal law as to general principles but not as to particular specifications of particular matters, although such specifications belong to the eternal law. And so human reason needs to proceed further to determine the particular prescriptions of human law.

Reply Obj. 2. Human reason as such is not the rule of things, but the first principles implanted by nature in human reason are the general rules or

---

[16]I–II, Q. 90, A. 1.   [17]Aristotle, *Metaphysics* X, 1 (1053a31–b3).   [18]Ibid.
[19]*On Free Choice* I, 6 and 15 (PL 32:1229, 1238).   [20]I–II, Q. 90, A. 1, *ad* 2.
[21]Ibid.   [22]I–II, Q. 9, AA. 2, 3, 4.   [23]*Rhetoric* II, 53.

measures of everything related to human conduct. And natural reason is the rule and measure of such things, although not of things from nature.

Reply Obj. 3. Practical reason regards practical matters, which are particular and contingent, and does not regard necessary things, as theoretical reason does. And so human laws cannot have the absolute certainty of demonstrated scientific conclusions. Nor need every measure be unerring and certain in every respect. Rather, every measure needs to be such only to the extent possible in its kind of thing.

FOURTH ARTICLE
Did Human Beings Need a Divine Law?

We thus proceed to the fourth inquiry. It seems that human beings did not need any divine law, for the following reasons:

Objection 1. The natural law is our participation in the eternal law, as I have said.[24] But eternal law is divine law, as I have said.[25] Therefore, we do not need another divine law besides the natural law and the human laws derived from natural law.

Obj. 2. Sir. 15:14 says that "God left human beings in the hands of their own deliberation." But deliberation is an act of reason, as I have maintained before.[26] Therefore, God left human beings to the governance of their own reason. But the dictates of human reason are human laws, as I have said.[27] Therefore, human beings do not need to be governed by another divine law.

Obj. 3. Human nature is more self-sufficient than irrational creatures. But irrational creatures have no divine law besides the inclinations that nature implants in them. Therefore, much less should rational creatures have a divine law besides the natural law.

On the contrary, David petitioned God to lay out the law before him, saying in Ps. 119:33: "Teach me the law, O Lord, in the way of your statutes."

I answer that in addition to the natural law and human laws, divine law was necessary to give direction to human life. And there are four reasons for this.

First, indeed, law directs our acts in relation to our ultimate end. And human beings, if they were indeed ordained only for an end that did not surpass the proportion of their natural ability, would not, regarding reason, need to have any direction superior to the natural law and human laws derived from the natural law. But because human beings are ordained for the end of eternal blessedness, which surpasses their proportional natural

---

[24]A. 2.   [25]A. 1.   [26]I–II, Q. 14, A. 1.   [27]A. 3.

human capacity, as I have maintained before,[28] God needed to lay down a law superior to the natural law and human laws to direct human beings to their end.

Second, because of the uncertainty of human judgment, especially regarding contingent and particular matters, different persons may judge differently about various human actions, and so even different and contrary laws result. Therefore, in order that human beings can know beyond any doubt what they should do or should not do, a divinely revealed law, regarding which error is impossible, was needed to direct human beings in their actions.

Third, human beings can make laws regarding things they are able to judge. But human beings can judge only sensibly perceptible external acts, not hidden internal movements. And yet human beings need to live righteously regarding both kinds of acts in order to attain complete virtue. And so human laws could not prohibit or adequately ordain internal acts, and divine law needed to supplement human laws.

Fourth, human laws cannot punish or prohibit all evil deeds, as Augustine says in his work *On Free Choice*.[29] This is because in seeking to eliminate all evils, one would thereby also take away many goods and not benefit the common good necessary for human companionship. Therefore, in order that no evil remain unforbidden or unpunished, there needed to be a divine law forbidding all sins.

And Ps. 19:7 touches on these four reasons when it says: "The law of the Lord is pure," that is, permitting no sinful wickedness; "converting souls," since it directs both external and internal acts; "the Lord's faithful witness" because of its certain truth and rectitude; "offering wisdom to the little ones," since it ordains human beings for a supernatural and divine end.

Reply Obj. 1. The natural law partakes of the eternal law in proportion to the capacity of human nature. But human beings need to be directed in a higher way to their ultimate supernatural end. And so God gives an additional law that partakes of the eternal law in a higher way.

Reply Obj. 2. Deliberation is an inquiry, and so deliberation needs to advance from some principles. And it does not suffice that it advance from first principles implanted by nature, that is, precepts of the natural law, for the aforementioned reasons.[30] Rather, other principles, namely, precepts of divine law, need to be supplied.

---

[28] I–II, Q. 5, A. 5.   [29] *On Free Choice* I, 5 (PL 32:1228).   [30] In the body of the article.

Reply Obj. 3. Irrational creatures are not ordained for higher ends than those proportioned to their natural powers. And so the argument of the objection is inapplicable.

FIFTH ARTICLE
Is There Only One Divine Law?

We thus proceed to the fifth inquiry. It seems that there is only one divine law, for the following reasons:

Objection 1. There is one set of laws of one king in one kingdom. But the whole human race is related to God as one king, as Ps. 47:7 says: "God is king of all the earth." Therefore, there is only one divine law.

Obj. 2. Every law is ordained for the end the lawmaker intends regarding those subject to the law. But God intends one and the same thing regarding all human beings, as 1 Tim. 2:4 says: "He wills all human beings to be saved and to come to the knowledge of the truth." Therefore, there is only one divine law.

Obj. 3. The divine law seems to approximate the eternal law, which is one, more than the natural law does, as the revelation of grace is higher than the knowledge of nature. But there is one natural law for all human beings. Therefore, much more is there one divine law for them.

On the contrary, the Apostle says in Heb. 7:12: "Since the priesthood has been transferred, the law needed to be changed." But the priesthood is twofold, namely, the priesthood of Leviticus and the priesthood of Christ, as Heb. 7:11 says. Therefore, there are two divine laws, namely, the Old Law and the New Law.

I answer that division causes number, as I said in the First Part.[31] And we distinguish things in two ways: in one way as things are altogether specifically different (e.g., horses and oxen); in a second way as the complete and the incomplete in the same species (e.g., adults and children). And it is in the latter way that we distinguish divine law into the Old and the New Law. And so the Apostle in Gal. 3:24-25 compares the condition of the Old Law to that of a child subject to a tutor, and the condition of the New Law to an adult no longer subject to a tutor.

And we note the perfection and imperfection of the two Laws by three things belonging to the divine law, as I have said before.[32] For in the first place, it belongs to any law to be directed to the common good as its end, as I have said before.[33] And this common good can be of two kinds. It may be a sensibly perceptible and earthly good, and the Old Law was

---

[31] I, Q. 30, A. 3.   [32] I–II: Q. 90, A. 2; Q. 90, A. 3, *ad* 2; Q. 91, A. 4.   [33] I–II, Q. 90, A. 2.

directly ordained for such a good. And so the people were invited at the very institution of the Old Law to occupy the earthly kingdom of the Canaanites.³⁴ Or the common good may be an intelligible and heavenly good, and the New Law ordains human beings for such a good. And so Christ at the very outset of his preaching invited human beings to the kingdom of heaven, saying: "Repent, for the kingdom of heaven is at hand."³⁵ And so Augustine says in his work *Against Faustus* that "the Old Testament contains promises of temporal things and so is called old, but the promise of eternal life belongs to the New Testament."³⁶

Second, it belongs to the divine law to direct human acts regarding the order of righteousness. And the New Law surpasses the Old Law in this respect by ordaining internal spiritual acts, as Mt. 5:20 says: "Unless your righteousness exceeds that of the Scribes and Pharisees, you will not enter the kingdom of heaven." And so there is the saying that "the Old Law stays our hand, the New Law stays our spirit."³⁷

Third, it belongs to the divine law to induce human beings to observe the commandments. And the Old Law indeed accomplished this by fear of punishments, while the New Law accomplishes this by love, which the grace of Christ, foreshadowed in the Old Law and conferred in the New Law, pours into our hearts. And so Augustine says in his work *Against Adimantus, Disciple of Mani* that "there is a little difference between the Law and the Gospel, namely, the difference between fear and love."³⁸

Reply Obj. 1. As the head of a household issues different commands to children and adults, so also the one king, God, in his one kingdom gave one law to human beings still imperfect and another more perfect law to those already led by the former law to a greater capacity for divine things.

Reply Obj. 2. Only Christ could save human beings, as Acts 4:12 says: "There is no other name given to human beings wherein we should be saved." And so a law completely leading all human beings to salvation could be given only after the coming of Christ. But a law containing rudiments of salvific righteousness needed to be given beforehand to the people from whom Christ was to be born, in order to prepare them to receive him.

Reply Obj. 3. The natural law directs human beings by certain general precepts in relation to which both the perfect and the imperfect are the same, and so the natural law is one and the same for everyone. But divine

---

³⁴Ex. 3:8–17.   ³⁵Mt. 4:17.   ³⁶*Against Faustus* IV, 2 (PL 42:217–18).
³⁷Cf. Peter Lombard, *Sentences* III, dist. 40, c. 1.   ³⁸*Against Adimantus, Disciple of Mani* 17 (PL 42:159). The "little difference" alludes to the fact that the Latin word for fear (*timor*) has one more letter than the Latin word for love (*amor*).

law also directs human beings regarding particular matters, for which the perfect and the imperfect are not similarly disposed. And so there needed to be two divine laws, as I have already said.[39]

SIXTH ARTICLE
Is There a Law of Concupiscence?

We thus proceed to the sixth inquiry. It seems that there is no law of concupiscence, for the following reasons:

Objection 1. Isidore says in his *Etymologies* that "law is based on reason."[40] But concupiscence is not based on reason. Rather, concupiscence deviates from reason. Therefore, concupiscence does not have the nature of law.

Obj. 2. Every law obliges, so that we call those who do not observe it transgressors. But concupiscence does not render persons transgressors because they do not follow its inclinations. Rather, concupiscence renders persons transgressors if they do. Therefore, concupiscence does not have the nature of law.

Obj. 3. Law is ordained for the common good, as I have maintained before.[41] But concupiscence does not incline us to the common good. Rather, concupiscence inclines us to private good. Therefore, concupiscence does not have the nature of law.

On the contrary, the Apostle says in Rom. 7:23: "I perceive another law in my bodily members repugnant to the law of my mind."

I answer that law belongs essentially to those who rule and measure, and by participation to the ruled and measured, as I have said before.[42] And so we call every inducement or ordination in things subject to law, law by participation, as is evident from what I have said before.[43] But in things subject to law, there can be inducements from the lawmaker in two ways. There are inducements in one way insofar as lawmakers directly induce their subjects to things, and sometimes different subjects to different actions. And we can accordingly speak of one law for soldiers and another law for merchants. There are inducements in a second way insofar as lawmakers indirectly induce their subjects to things, namely, insofar as lawmakers by depriving subjects of some office transfer them to another position in society and to another law, as it were. For example, if a soldier should be discharged from the army, he will be transferred to the law governing farmers or merchants.

---

[39] In the body of the article.   [40] *Etymologies* V, 3 (PL 82:199).   [41] I–II, Q. 90, A. 2.   [42] A. 2; I–II, Q. 90, A. 1, *ad* 1.   [43] Ibid.

Therefore, God, the lawmaker, subjects different creatures to different inducements, so that what is in one way law for one kind of creature, is in another way contrary to law for another kind of creature. This is as if I should say that ferocity is in one way the law for dogs but in another way contrary to the law for sheep or other meek animals.

Therefore, it is the law for human beings, which is allotted by God's ordination according to their condition, that they act according to reason. And this law was indeed so effective in our first condition that nothing outside reason or contrary to reason could come upon Adam surreptiously. But when Adam withdrew from God, he fell subject to the impulses of his sense appetites. And this also happens in particular to each human being the more the individual has withdrawn from reason, so that the individual in a way resembles beasts, who are borne along by the impulses of their sense appetites. Just so, Ps. 49:20 says: "Human beings, although they were in a condition of honor, did not understand; they have been paired with mindless beasts and became like them."

Therefore, in other animals, the very inclinations of sense appetites, which we call concupiscence, indeed directly have the nature of law in an absolute sense, although in the way we can speak of law in such things. And in human beings, such inclinations of sense appetites do not have the nature of law. Rather, they are deviations from the law of reason. But since divine justice stripped human beings of original justice and the full force of reason, the very impulses of sense appetites that impel human beings have the nature of law, since such impulses are a punishment and the result of divine law depriving human beings of their dignity.

Reply Obj. 1. The argument of this objection is valid regarding concupiscence considered as such, as it inclines us to evil. For concupiscence does not have the nature of law in this way, as I have said,[44] but has the nature of law insofar as it results from the justice of divine law. This is as if we were to say that the law allows nobles to be put to servile work because of their misdeeds.

Reply Obj. 2. The argument of this objection is valid regarding law as a rule or measure. For those deviating from the law are thus constituted transgressors of the law. But concupiscence is not a law in this sense. Rather, concupiscence is a law by a participation, as I have said before.[45]

---

[44] In the body of the article.   [45] Ibid.

Reply Obj. 3. The argument of this objection is valid about concupiscence as to its own inclinations but not as to its origin. And yet if we were to consider the inclinations of sense appetites as they exist in other animals, then the inclinations are ordained for the common good, that is, the preservation of nature specifically and individually. And this is also true regarding human beings insofar as their sense appetites are subject to reason. But we are talking about concupiscence insofar as it departs from the ordination of reason.

QUESTION 92

On the Effects of Law

FIRST ARTICLE
Is the Effect of Law to Make Human Beings Good?

We thus proceed to the first inquiry. It seems that it does not belong to law to make human beings good, for the following reasons:

Objection 1. Virtue makes human beings good, since "virtue makes those possessing it good," as the *Ethics* says.[1] But human beings have virtue only from God, since he "produces virtue in us apart from our efforts,"[2] as I have said before regarding the definition of virtue.[3] Therefore, it does not belong to law to make human beings good.

Obj. 2. Law benefits human beings only if they obey law. But goodness causes human beings to obey law. Therefore, human beings first need goodness in order to obey law. Therefore, law does not make them good.

Obj. 3. Law is ordained for the common good, as I have said.[4] But some ill disposed regarding their own good are well disposed regarding what belongs to the common good. Therefore, it does not belong to law to make human beings good.

Obj. 4. Some laws are tyrannical, as the Philosopher says in the *Politics*.[5] But a tyrant strives for his own good, not the good of his subjects. Therefore, it does not belong to law to make human beings good.

On the contrary, the Philosopher says in the *Ethics* that it is "the will of every lawmaker to make his citizens good."[6]

I answer that, as I have said before,[7] law is simply a ruler's dictate of reason that governs his subjects. And the virtue of every subject is to be duly subject to the ruler. Just so, we perceive that the the virtue of the irascible and concupiscible powers consists of being duly obedient to reason. And accordingly, "the virtue of every subject consists of being duly subject to the ruler," as the Philosopher says in the *Politics*.[8] And every law is ordained to be obeyed by those subject to it. And so it evidently belongs to law to induce subjects to their requisite virtue. Therefore, since virtue makes those possessing it good, the proper effect of law is

---

[1] Aristotle, *Ethics* II, 6 (1106a15–16).   [2] Cf. Peter Lombard, *Sentences* II, dist. 27, c. 5.   [3] I–II, Q. 55, A. 4.   [4] I–II, Q. 90, A. 2.   [5] *Politics* III, 6 (1282b12).   [6] *Ethics* II, 1 (1103b3–4).   [7] I–II, Q. 90, A. 1, *ad* 2; AA. 3, 4.   [8] *Politics* I, 5 (1260a20–24).

consequently to make its subjects good, either absolutely or in some respect. For if the aim of the lawmaker strives for real good, that is, the common good regulated by divine justice, law consequently makes human beings absolutely good. But if the aim of lawmakers is set upon what is not absolutely good but what is useful or desirable for themselves or contrary to divine justice, then law makes human beings relatively, not absolutely, good, namely, in relation to such a regime. So also does good belong to things in themselves evil. For example, we speak of a good robber, since he acts suitably to accomplish his end.

Reply Obj. 1. There are two kinds of virtue, namely, acquired virtues and infused virtues, as is evident from what I have said before.[9] And habitual action contributes something to both but in different ways. For habitual action causes acquired virtue, and disposes persons to receive infused virtue, and preserves and augments infused virtues already possessed. And because laws are laid down to direct human actions, law makes human beings good as much as their actions conduce to virtue. And so also the Philosopher says in the *Politics* that "lawmakers make subjects good by habituating them to good deeds."[10]

Reply Obj. 2. People do not always obey law out of the perfect goodness of virtue. Rather, they sometimes indeed obey law out of fear of punishment and sometimes only out of dictates of reason, which cause virtue, as I have maintained before.[11]

Reply Obj. 3. We weigh the goodness of any part in relation to the whole to which it belongs. And so also Augustine says in his *Confessions* that "every part is base that is in discord with the whole to which it belongs."[12] Therefore, since every human being is part of a political community, no human being can be good unless rightly related to the common good. Nor can a whole be rightly constituted except by parts rightly related to it. And so the common good of a political community can be rightly disposed only if its citizens, at least those to whom its ruling belongs, are virtuous. But it suffices as regards the good of the community that other citizens be virtuous enough to obey the commands of the law. And so the Philosopher says in the *Politics* that "the virtue of a ruler and that of a good man are the same, but the virtue of any ordinary citizen and that of a good man are not."[13]

Reply Obj. 4. A tyrannical law, since it is not in accord with reason, is not a law, absolutely speaking. Rather, it is a perversion of law. And yet such a law strives to make citizens good inasmuch as it partakes of the

---

[9]I–II, Q. 63, A. 2.   [10]Actually, *Ethics* II, 1 (1103b3–4).   [11]I–II, Q. 63, A. 1.   [12]*Confessions* III, 8 (PL 32:689).   [13]*Politics* III, 2 (1277a20–23).

nature of law. For it only partakes of the nature of law insofar as it is a ruler's dictate for his subjects and strives to make them duly obedient, that is, to make them good in relation to such a regime, not absolutely good.

SECOND ARTICLE
Do We Suitably Designate Legal Acts?

We thus proceed to the second inquiry. It seems that we do not suitably designate legal acts to consist of "commanding, forbidding, permitting, and punishing,"[14] for the following reasons:

Objection 1. "Every law is a general precept," as the Jurist says.[15] But giving a command is the same as laying down a precept. Therefore, the other three things are superfluous.

Obj. 2. The effect of law is to induce subjects to good, as I have said before.[16] But counsel concerns a higher good than precept concerns. Therefore, counsel belongs more to law than precept does.

Obj. 3. As punishment spurs human beings to good deeds, so also do rewards. Therefore, as we reckon punishment an effect of law, so also should we reckon reward.

Obj. 4. A lawmaker aims to make human beings good, as I have said before.[17] But those who obey law only out of fear of punishment are not good, since "although some do good out of servile fear, which is fear of punishment, they do not do it rightly," as Augustine says.[18] Therefore, it does not seem to belong to law to punish.

On the contrary, Isidore says in his *Etymologies:* "Every law either permits something (e.g., that a brave man may ask for a reward) or prohibits something (e.g., that no one is permitted to seek marriage with a consecrated virgin) or punishes something (e.g., that murderers be beheaded)."[19]

I answer that as assertions are dictates of reason by way of declaring things, so also laws are dictates of reason by way of commanding things. But it belongs to reason to lead us from some things to other things. And so, as reason in the case of demonstrative sciences leads us to assent to conclusions from certain first principles, so also reason leads us to assent to legal precepts from knowledge of some things.

And legal precepts concern human actions, which law directs, as I have said before.[20] And there are three kinds of human acts. For as I have said before,[21] some human acts are good by their nature, that is, virtuous. And

---

[14] Justinian, *Digest* I, title 3, law 7.   [15] Ibid. I, title 3, law 1.   [16] A. 1.
[17] Ibid.   [18] *Against the Two Letters of Pelagius* II, 9, n. 21 (PL 44:586).
[19] *Etymologies* V, 19 (PL 82:202).   [20] I–II: Q. 90, AA. 1, 2; Q. 91, A. 4. [21] I–II, Q. 18, A. 8.

laws are supposed to prescribe or command such acts, since "laws command every kind of virtuous act," as the *Ethics* says.[22] And some human acts are evil by their nature, that is, vicious. And laws are supposed to forbid such acts. And some human acts are morally indifferent by reason of their kind. And laws are supposed to permit such acts. And we can call all slightly good or slightly evil human acts morally indifferent.

But fear of punishment is what law makes use of to induce obedience, and we in this respect posit punishment as an effect of law.

Reply Obj. 1. As desisting from evil partakes of the nature of good, so also prohibitions partake of the nature of precept. And so, understanding "precept" broadly, we call every law a precept.

Reply Obj. 2. Counseling is not a peculiar function of law. Rather, counseling falls also within the competence of private persons, who are without competence to establish law. And so also the Apostle, in proposing to give a counsel, says in 1 Cor. 7:12: "I, not the Lord, make this statement." And so we do not posit counseling among the effects of law.

Reply Obj. 3. Anyone is competent to bestow rewards, but only administrators of law, under the authority of which punishments are inflicted, are competent to punish. And so we posit only punishments, not rewards, as legal acts.

Reply Obj. 4. By beginning to become habituated to avoid evil deeds and to do good deeds out of fear of punishment, persons are sometimes brought to behave in such a way with pleasure and of their own will. And so law even by inflicting punishments induces human beings to be good.

---

[22] Aristotle, *Ethics* V, 1 (1129b19–23).

QUESTION 93
On the Eternal Law

FIRST ARTICLE
Is the Eternal Law a Supreme Plan[1] in God?

We thus proceed to the first inquiry. It seems that the eternal law is not a supreme plan in God, for the following reasons:

Objection 1. There is only one eternal law. But there are many natures of things in the mind of God, for Augustine says in his work *Eighty-Three Questions* that "God made each thing with its own nature[2]."[3] Therefore, the eternal law is not the same as the plan in his mind.

Obj. 2. It belongs to the nature of law that it be promulgated in words, as I have said before.[4] But regarding divine things, we speak of the Word as person, as I maintained in the First Part,[5] but we speak of the divine plan as belonging to God essentially. Therefore, the eternal law is not the same as the divine plan.

Obj. 3. Augustine says in his work *On True Religion:* "We perceive that there is a law superior to our minds, a law we call truth."[6] But the law superior to our minds is the eternal law. Therefore, truth is the eternal law. But the nature of truth is not the same as the nature of a plan. Therefore, the eternal law is not the same as a supreme plan.

On the contrary, Augustine says in his work *On Free Choice* that "the eternal law is the supreme plan that we should always obey."[7]

I answer that as there preexists in every craftsman a plan for the things produced by his skill, so also there needs to exist in every ruler an orderly plan for the things his subjects ought to do. And as we call the plan for the things that a craft produces, the craft or ideal type of the things crafted, so also the plan of a ruler for his subjects' actions has the nature

---

[1] In ST I, Q. 15, A. 2, Thomas Aquinas uses "*ratio*" to signify God's "idea" of the order of the whole universe. This "idea" in connection with creation evidently constitutes a plan, and I translate "ratio" in this context accordingly.   [2] Each kind of thing has a proper nature or essence. Both Augustine and Aquinas use "*ratio*" to signify the natures or essences of things as "ideas" in God's mind. Cf. ST I, Q. 15, A. 2. Also see Glossary, s.v. "Essence."   [3] *Eighty-Three Questions,* Q. 46, n. 2 (PL 40:30).   [4] I–II, Q. 90, A. 4; Q. 91, A. 1, *ad* 2.   [5] I, Q. 34, A. 1.   [6] *On True Religion* 30 (PL 34:147).   [7] *On Free Choice* I, 6, n. 15 (PL 32:1229).

of law, provided that the other conditions that I cited before regarding the nature of law[8] are observed. And God in his wisdom creates all things and is related to them like a craftman to the products of his craft, as I have maintained in the First Part.[9] God also governs all the actions and movements in particular kinds of creatures, as I have likewise maintained in the First Part.[10] And so, as the plan of divine wisdom has the nature of a craft or type or idea because all things are created through it, so the plan of divine wisdom causing the movement of all things to their requisite ends has the nature of law. And so the eternal law is simply the plan of divine wisdom that directs all the actions and movements of created things.

Reply Obj. 1. Augustine is speaking in the cited text about ideal natures, which regard the requisite natures of particular things. And so these types have some diversity and plurality regarding their different relations to things, as I have maintained in the First Part.[11] But we speak of law directing actions in relation to the common good, as I have said before.[12] And we consider things in themselves diverse as one insofar as they are ordained for the common good. And so there is one eternal law, which is this orderly plan.

Reply Obj. 2. We can consider two things regarding any word, namely, the word itself and what the word expresses. For example, spoken words are utterances from the mouths of human beings, and these words express what the words signify. And mental words, which are simply the mental concepts whereby human beings express mentally the things about which they are thinking, have the same nature. Therefore, regarding divine things, we speak of the Word itself, which the Father's understanding conceives, as the Second Person of the Trinity, and this Word expresses everything in the Father's knowledge, whether things proper to God's essence or things proper to each Person or things created by God, as Augustine makes evident in his work *On the Trinity.*[13] And among other things so expressed, the Word itself also expresses the eternal law itself. But it does not follow that we speak of the eternal law as the Second Person of the Trinity, although we appropriate the eternal law to the Son because of the appropriateness of the divine plan for the Word.

Reply Obj. 3. The nature of the divine intellect is otherwise related to things than the nature of the human mind is. For things are the measure of the human mind, that is to say, we call human concepts true because they are in accord with things, not because of the concepts themselves,

---

[8]I–II, Q. 90.   [9]I, Q. 14, A. 8.   [10]I, Q. 103, A. 5.   [11]I, Q. 15, A. 2.
[12]I–II, Q. 90, A. 2.   [13]*On the Trinity* XV, 14 (PL 42:1076).

since "opinions are true or false because things are or are not such."[14] But the divine intellect is the measure of things, since everything has as much truth as it is modeled on the divine intellect, as I have maintained in the First Part.[15] And so the divine intellect is true in itself. And so its nature is truth itself.

SECOND ARTICLE
Do All Know the Eternal Law?

We thus proceed to the second inquiry. It seems that not everybody knows the eternal law, for the following reasons:

Objection 1. The Apostle says in 1 Cor. 2:11: "Only the Spirit of God knows the things proper to God." But the eternal law is a plan in God's mind. Therefore, no one but God knows the eternal law.

Obj. 2. Augustine says in his work *On Free Choice:* "The eternal law is that by which it is right that all things be most orderly."[16] But not everybody knows how all things are most orderly. Therefore, not everybody knows the eternal law.

Obj. 3. Augustine says in his work *On True Religion* that "human beings cannot judge regarding the eternal law."[17] But "everyone judges rightly about things one knows," as the *Ethics* says.[18] Therefore, we do not know the eternal law.

On the contrary, Augustine says in his work *On Free Choice* that "knowledge of the eternal law is imprinted on us."[19]

I answer that we can know things in two ways: in one way in themselves; in a second way in their effects, which are like the things. For example, those who are not looking at the sun know it in the effects of its rays. Therefore, we should say no one except the blessed, who see God by his essence, can know the eternal law as it is in itself. But every rational creature knows it in some of its radiating effects, whether greater or lesser effects. For every knowledge of truth is a radiation and participation of eternal law, which is incommunicable truth, as Augustine says in his work *On True Religion.*[20] For everybody knows truth to some extent, at least regarding the general principles of the natural law. But some share more and some less in knowing truth regarding other things. And so also they know more or less of the eternal law.

---

[14] Aristotle, *Categories* 4 (2a7–8).   [15] I, Q. 16, A. 1.   [16] *On Free Choice* I, 6, n. 15 (PL 32:1229).   [17] *On True Religion* 31 (PL 34:148).   [18] Aristotle, *Ethics* I, 3 (1094b27–1095a2).   [19] *On Free Choice* I, 6, n. 15 (PL 32:1229). [20] *On True Religion* 31 (PL 34:147).

Reply Obj. 1. We indeed cannot know things proper to God in themselves, but such things are evident to us in their effects, as Rom. 1:20 says: "We perceive the invisible things of God when they are understood through the things he created."

Reply Obj. 2. Although everyone knows the eternal law according to one's capacity, in the aforementioned way, no one can know it comprehensively, since its effects cannot completely reveal it. And so it is not necessary that those who know the eternal law in the aforementioned way know the whole order of things, whereby all things are most orderly.

Reply Obj. 3. Judging about things can be understood in two ways. Judging about things can be understood in one way as a cognitive power judges regarding its own object, as Job 12:11 says: "Do not ears discern words, and diners' taste buds discern taste?" And the Philosopher in this way of judging says that "everyone judges rightly things that one knows," namely, in judging whether a proposition is true. We can understand judging in a second way as superiors judge about subordinates by practical judgments, namely, whether subordinates should or should not be such and such. And no one can judge about the eternal law in that way.

THIRD ARTICLE

Is Every Law Derived from the Eternal Law?

We thus proceed to the third inquiry. It seems that not every law is derived from the eternal law, for the following reasons:

Objection 1. There is a law of concupiscence, as I have said before.[21] But that law is not derived from divine law, that is, eternal law, since wisdom of the flesh, which the Apostle in Rom. 8:7 says "cannot be subject to the law of God," belongs to the law of concupiscence. Therefore, not every law comes from the eternal law.

Obj. 2. Nothing evil can come from the eternal law, since "eternal law is that whereby it is right that all things be most orderly,"[22] as I have said before.[23] But some laws are evil, as Is. 10:1 says: "Woe to those who make wicked laws." Therefore, not every law comes from the eternal law.

Obj. 3. Augustine says in his work *On Free Choice* that "laws prescribed for ruling a people rightly permit many things that divine providence punishes."[24] But the plan of divine providence is the eternal law, as I have said.[25] Therefore, not every right law comes from the eternal law.

---

[21] I–II, Q. 91, A. 6.   [22] Augustine, *On Free Choice* I, 6, n. 15 (PL 32:1229).
[23] A. 2, obj. 2.   [24] *On Free Choice* I, 5, n. 13 (PL 32:1228).   [25] A. 1.

On the contrary, Divine wisdom in Prov. 8:15 says: "Kings rule by me, and lawmakers discern what is just." But the plan of divine wisdom is the eternal law, as I have said before.[26] Therefore, all laws derive from the eternal law.

I answer that Law signifies a plan directing acts to an end, as I have said before.[27] But in the case of all interrelated causes, the power of a secondary cause needs to be derived from the power of the primary cause, since a secondary cause causes only insofar as the primary cause moves the secondary cause. And so also we perceive the same regarding all who govern, that the chief ruler communicates his plan of government to secondary administrators. For example, a king communicates his plan for the affairs of a political community by issuing commands to subordinate administrators. And also in the case of things requiring the skill of craftsmen, a master builder communicates his plan for the activities requiring those skills to subordinate craftsmen, who carry out the manual work involved. Therefore, since the eternal law is the plan of government in the supreme ruler, all plans of government in subordinate rulers need to be derived from the eternal law. But such plans of subordinate government consist of all the other laws besides the eternal law. And so all laws are derived from the eternal law insofar as they partake of right reason. And so Augustine says in his work *On Free Choice* that "nothing is just or lawful in earthly laws that human beings have not derived for themselves from the eternal law."[28]

Reply Obj. 1. Concupiscence has the nature of law regarding human beings insofar as it is a punishment resulting from divine justice, and it is in this respect evidently derived from eternal law. But insofar as it inclines human beings to sin, it is contrary to God's law and does not have the nature of law, as is clear from what I have said before.[29]

Reply Obj. 2. Human law has the nature of law insofar as it is in accord with right reason, and then it is evidently derived from eternal law. But we call human law evil insofar as it withdraws from reason. And then it has the nature of brute force rather than of law. And yet insofar as some likeness of law is preserved in an evil law because one empowered to make law ordained it, it is also in this respect derived from the eternal law. For "every ruling power is from the Lord God," as Rom. 13:1 says.

Reply Obj. 3. We speak of human law permitting some things because it is unable to direct them, not because it approves them. But divine law directs many things that human law cannot, since more things are subject

---

[26]Ibid. 32:1229).   [27]I–II, Q. 90, AA. 1, 2.   [28]*On Free Choice* I, 6, n. 15 (PL
[29]I–II, Q. 91, A. 6.

to higher causes than to lower causes. And so the fact that human law is not imposed regarding things that it cannot direct, derives from the order of eternal law. But it would be otherwise if human law were to approve things that eternal law condemns. And so we conclude that human law cannot completely attain the eternal law, not that human law is not derived from eternal law.

FOURTH ARTICLE
Are Necessary and Eternal Things Subject to the Eternal Law?

We thus proceed to the fourth inquiry. It seems that necessary and eternal things are subject to the eternal law, for the following reasons:

Objection 1. Everything reasonable is subject to reason. But the divine will is reasonable, since it is just. Therefore, it is subject to reason. But the eternal law is the divine plan. Therefore, God's will is subject to the eternal law. But God's will is eternal. Therefore, eternal and necessary things are subject to the eternal law.

Obj. 2. Everything subject to a king is subject to the king's law. But the Son "will be subject to the God and Father, since the Son will hand over the kingdom to the Father," as 1 Cor. 15:24, 28 says. Therefore, the Son, who is eternal, is subject to the eternal law.

Obj. 3. The eternal law is the plan of divine providence. But there are many necessary things subject to divine providence (e.g., the permanence of spiritual substances and heavenly bodies). Therefore, even necessary things are subject to the eternal law.

On the contrary, necessary things cannot be disposed otherwise than they are, and so they do not need any restraint. But laws are imposed on human beings to restrain them from evil, as is evident from what I have said before.[30] Therefore, necessary things are not subject to the law.

I answer that the eternal law is the plan of divine governance, as I have said before.[31] Therefore, everything subject to divine governance is also subject to the eternal law, but things not subject to divine governance are not subject to the eternal law. And we can consider the distinction between the two kinds of things in regard to matters that concern us. For example, things that human beings can do are subject to human governance, but things that belong to the nature of human beings (e.g., that human beings have souls or hands or feet) are not subject to human governance. Therefore, everything belonging to created things, whether contingent or necessary, belongs to the eternal law, but things belonging to

---

[30] I–II, Q. 92, A. 2.   [31] A. 1.

the divine nature or essence are in fact the eternal law itself and not subject to the eternal law.

Reply Obj. 1. We can speak about God's will in two ways. We can speak about his will in one way regarding the will itself, and then his will, since it is his very essence, is the same as the eternal law and not subject to divine governance or the eternal law. We can speak of God's will in a second way as to the things God wills regarding creatures, things indeed subject to the eternal law, since the plan for them belongs to his wisdom. And we call God's will reasonable because of these things. Otherwise, considering his will itself, we should call it the very plan.

Reply Obj. 2. God does not make the Son of God but by nature begets him. And so the Son is not subject to divine providence or the eternal law. Rather, he is the eternal law by appropriation, as Augustine makes clear in his work *On True Religion*.[32] And we say that he is subject to the Father by reason of his human nature, and we say that the Father is greater than he in the same regard.[33]

Reply Obj. 3. We grant the argument of this objection, since it deals validly with created necessary things.

Reply Obj. 4.[34] As the Philosopher says in the *Metaphysics*,[35] the necessity of some necessary things is caused, and then they have from something else the fact that they cannot be otherwise than they are. And this is a most effective restraint, since we speak of restrained things being restrained insofar as they cannot do otherwise than they are disposed to do.

FIFTH ARTICLE
Are Contingent Natural Things Subject to the Eternal Law?

We thus proceed to the fifth inquiry. It seems that contingent natural things are not subject to the eternal law, for the following reasons:

Objection 1. Promulgation belongs to the nature of law, as I have said before.[36] But promulgation can be made only to rational creatures, to whom things can be declared. Therefore, only rational creatures are subject to the eternal law. Therefore, contingent natural things are not.

Obj. 2. "Things that obey reason partake of reason in some respect," as the *Ethics* says.[37] But the eternal law is a supreme plan, as I have said before.[38] Therefore, contingent natural things, since they are completely

---

[32] *On True Religion* 31 (PL 34:147).   [33] Jn. 14:28.   [34] This reply qualifies the argument in the section *On the contrary*.   [35] *Metaphysics* V, 5 (1015b10–15).   [36] I–II, Q. 90, A. 4.   [37] *Ethics* I, 13 (1102b25–28).   [38] A. 1.

irrational and do not in any way partake of reason, do not seem to be subject to the eternal law.

Obj. 3. The eternal law is most efficacious. But deficiencies occur in contingent natural things. Therefore, such things are not subject to the eternal law.

On the contrary, Prov. 8:29 says: "When he [God] set bounds to the sea and imposed a law on its waters not to transgress their limits."

I answer that we should speak about the law of human beings and the eternal law, the law of God, in different ways. For the law of human beings governs only rational creatures subject to human beings. And the reason for this is that law directs actions proper to those subject to another's governance. And so, strictly speaking, one does not impose a law on one's own actions. But all the things done regarding the use of irrational things subject to human beings are done by the actions of the very human beings causing the things done. For irrational creatures so used are acted upon by other things and do not act upon themselves, as I have maintained before.[39] And so human beings cannot impose law on irrational things, however much the latter are subject to the former. But human beings can impose law on rational beings subject to them, insofar as human beings by precepts or declarations communicate to their subjects rules to govern the subjects' actions.

And as human beings by their declarations imprint an inner source of action on other human beings subject to them, so also God imprints on all the things of nature the sources of their own activities. And so we say in this respect that God commands the whole of nature, as Ps. 148:6 says: "He established an ordinance, and it will not pass away." And all movements and actions of the whole of nature are also in this respect subject to the eternal law. And so irrational creatures, as directed by divine providence, not by understanding God's commands, are subject to the eternal law in a different way than rational creatures are.

Reply Obj. 1. The imprint of inner sources of activity is to natural things as promulgation of law is to human beings, since the promulgation of law imprints on human beings a source that directs their actions, as I have said.[40]

Reply Obj. 2. Irrational creatures do not partake of human reason, nor do they obey it, but they partake of God's reason by obeying it. For the power of God's reason extends to more things than the power of human reason does. And as members of the human body are moved at the command of human reason but do not partake of reason, since they do have

---

[39] I–II, Q. 1, A. 2.   [40] In the body of the article.

any cognition subordinated to reason, so also God causes the movements of irrational creatures, which are not on that account rational.

Reply Obj. 3. Deficiencies that occur in things of nature, although outside the order of particular causes, are not outside the order of universal causes, and especially of the first cause, that is, God, whose providence nothing can escape, as I have said in the First Part.[41] And because the eternal law is the plan of divine providence, as I have said,[42] so deficiencies of things of nature are subject to the eternal law.

SIXTH ARTICLE

Are All Human Affairs Subject to the Eternal Law?

We thus proceed to the sixth inquiry. It seems that not all human affairs are subject to the eternal law, for the following reasons:

Objection 1. The Apostle says in Gal. 5:18: "If the Spirit guides you, you are not under the law." But righteous human beings, who are children of God by adoption, are led by the Spirit of God, as Rom. 8:14 says: "Those led by the Spirit of God are children of God." Therefore, not every human being is under the eternal law.

Obj. 2. The Apostle says in Rom. 8:17: "The wisdom of the flesh is the enemy of God, since that wisdom is not subject to the law of God." But there are many human beings in whom wisdom of the flesh dominates. Therefore, not all human beings are subject to the eternal law, that is, the law of God.

Obj. 3. Augustine says in his work *On Free Choice* that "the eternal law is the means whereby the wicked merit unhappiness, and the virtuous a blessed life."[43] But human beings already blessed or already damned are not in a condition to merit. Therefore, such human beings are not subject to the eternal law.

On the contrary, Augustine says in *The City of God:* "Nothing is in any way withdrawn from the laws of the most high creator and lawgiver, who administers the peace of the universe."[44]

I answer that there are two ways in which things are subject to the eternal law, as is evident from what I have said before[45]: one way as things partake of the eternal law in a conscious way; a second way by acting and being acted upon as things partake of the eternal law by reason of causes acting on them. And irrational creatures are subject to the eternal law in the second way, as I have said.[46] But because rational natures, along with

---

[41] I, Q. 22, A. 2.　　　[42] A. 1.　　　[43] *On Free Choice* I, 6, n. 15 (PL 32:1229).
[44] *The City of God* XIX, 12 (PL 41:640).　　　[45] A. 5.　　　[46] Ibid.

what is common to all creatures, have something proper to them as rational, they are consequently subject to the eternal law in both ways. This is
because they know the eternal law in some regard, as I have said,[47] and
each rational creature has an inclination from nature toward things conso-
nant with the eternal law. For "we are by nature equipped to possess virtues," as the *Ethics* says.[48]

But both ways are indeed incomplete and in some regard destroyed in
the wicked, in whom both the natural inclination to virtue is perverted by
vicious habits, and the natural knowledge of goodness is darkened by
emotions and sinful habits. And both ways are more complete in the virtuous, since knowledge of faith and of wisdom is added to their natural
knowledge of goodness, and the inner causal activity of grace and virtue is
added to their natural inclination toward goodness.

Therefore, the virtuous are completely subject to the eternal law, as
they always act in accord with it. And the wicked are indeed incompletely
subject to the eternal law regarding their own actions, as they incompletely recognize and incompletely incline to goodness. But what their
actions lack is proportionately supplemented by what they undergo,
namely, as they suffer what the eternal law dictates for them insofar as
they fail to do what befits the eternal law. And so Augustine says in his
work *On Free Choice* : "I think that the righteous act subject to the eternal
law."[49] And he says in his work *On Catechizing the Uneducated* that "God
knows how to supply the inferior parts of his creation with the most suitable laws, by the just wretchedness of souls that abandon him."[50]

Reply Obj. 1. We can understand the words of the Apostle in two ways.
We can understand them in one way as we understand to be under the
law those who are subject to the obligations of the law against their will,
as if pinned down by a weight. And so a gloss on the cited text says that
"those are under the law who abstain from evil deeds out of fear of the
punishment that the law threatens, not out of the love of justice."[51] And
in this sense, spiritual human beings are not under the law, since they
willingly fulfill the obligations of the law by the charity that the Holy
Spirit pours into their hearts.

We can understand the words of the Apostle in a second way as we say
that the deeds of human beings led by the Holy Spirit are deeds of the
Spirit rather than deeds of the human beings. And so since the Holy
Spirit, like the Son, is not subject to the law, as I have said before,[52] such

---

[47] A. 2.   [48] Aristotle, *Ethics* II, 1 (1103a25–26).   [49] *On Free Choice* I,
15, n. 31 (PL 32:1238).   [50] *On Catechizing the Uneducated* 18 (PL 40:333).
[51] *Glossa ordinaria*, on Gal. 5:18 (PL 114:584); Peter Lombard, *Glossa*, on Gal.
5:18 (PL 192:158–59).   [52] A. 4, *ad* 2.

deeds, as they belong to the Holy Spirit, are as a result not under the law. And the Apostle attests to this, saying in 2 Cor. 3:17: "Where there is the Spirit of the Lord, there is freedom."

Reply Obj. 2. Wisdom of the flesh cannot be subject to the law of God regarding resulting actions, since that wisdom inclines human beings to actions contrary to his law. But it can be subject to the law of God regarding what human beings undergo as a result, since it deserves to suffer punishment by the law of divine justice.

Nonetheless, wisdom of the flesh does not so dominate in any human being that the whole goodness of nature is destroyed. And so human beings retain an inclination to do the things that belong to the eternal law. For I have maintained before that sin does not take away the whole goodness of nature.[53]

Reply Obj. 3. The same cause preserves things when they reach their end and inclines them to it. For example, the weight of heavy things causes them to rest in lower places and to be moved thither. And so we should say that as the eternal law causes persons to merit blessedness or wretchedness, so the same law causes them to be preserved in blessedness or wretchedness. And both the blessed and the damned are in this way subject to the eternal law.

---

[53] I–II, Q. 85, A. 2.

QUESTION 94
On the Natural Law

FIRST ARTICLE
Is the Natural Law a Habit?

We thus proceed to the first inquiry. It seems that the natural law is a habit, for the following reasons:

Objection 1. "Three things belong to the soul: powers, habits, and emotions," as the Philosopher says in the *Ethics*.[1] But the natural law is neither a power of the soul nor an emotion. Therefore, the natural law is a habit.

Obj. 2. Basil says that conscience, that is, *synderesis*, is "the law of our intellect,"[2] and we can only understand such regarding the natural law. But *synderesis* is a habit, as I maintained in the First Part.[3] Therefore, the natural law is a habit.

Obj. 3. The natural law always abides in human beings, as I shall make clear later.[4] But human beings' reason, to which that law belongs, is not always thinking about the natural law. Therefore, the natural law is a habit, not an act.

On the contrary, Augustine says in his work *On the Marital Good* that "habits are the means whereby we do things when we need to."[5] But the natural law is not such, since that law belongs to infants and the damned, who cannot act by reason of its presence. Therefore, the natural law is not a habit.

I answer that we can speak about habits in two ways. We speak of them in one way in the strict sense and essentially, and then the natural law is not a habit. For I have said before that the natural law is constituted by reason,[6] just as propositions are works of reason. And what one does, and the means whereby one does it, are not the same. For example, one makes a fitting speech by means of the habit of grammar. Therefore, since habits are the means whereby one does things, the natural law cannot be a habit in the strict sense and essentially.

We can speak of habits in a second way as what we possess by reason of habits. For example, we call faith what we have by reason of the habit of

---

[1] *Ethics* II, 5 (1105b20–21).   [2] *On the Six Days of Creation,* homily 7, n. 5 (PG 29:157).   [3] I, Q. 79, A. 12.   [4] A. 6.   [5] *On the Marital Good* 21 (PL 40:390).   [6] I–II, Q. 90, A. 1, *ad* 2.

faith. And so, as reason sometimes actually considers precepts of the natural law and sometimes only habitually possesses them, we can in the latter way say that the natural law is a habit. Just so, the indemonstrable first principles in theoretical matters are principles belonging to the habit of first principles, not the very habit.

Reply Obj. 1. The Philosopher in the cited text is attempting to discover the genus of virtues. And since virtues are evidently sources of activity, he posits only things that are sources of human activity, namely, powers, habits, and emotions. But other things belong to the soul besides the latter three. For example, certain acts belong to the soul: willing to those willing, and things known to those knowing. And the natural properties of the soul, such as immortality and the like, belong to the soul.

Reply Obj. 2. Basil calls *synderesis* the law of our intellect insofar as it is the habit that contains the precepts of the natural law, that is, the first principles of human actions.

Reply Obj. 3. The argument of this objection reaches the conclusion that we possess the natural law in a habitual way, and we concede this.

Qualification of the argument in the section On the contrary. Sometimes, due to an impediment, one cannot make use of what one possesses habitually. For example, human beings cannot make use of habitual knowledge when they are asleep. And likewise, children cannot make use of habitual understanding of first principles, or even of the natural law, which they possess habitually, due to their immature age.

SECOND ARTICLE
Does the Natural Law Include Several Precepts or Only One?

We thus proceed to the second inquiry. It seems that that the natural law includes only one precept, not several, for the following reasons:

Objection 1. Law belongs to the genus of precept, as I have maintained before.[7] Therefore, if there were to be many precepts of the natural law, it would follow logically that there would also be many natural laws.

Obj. 2. The natural law results from the nature of human beings. But human nature as a whole is one, although multiple regarding its parts. Therefore, either there is only one precept of the natural law because of the unity of the whole, or there are many precepts because of the many parts of human nature. And so even things that regard inclinations of concupiscible power will need to belong to the natural law.

---

[7] I–II, Q. 92, A. 2.

Obj. 3. Law belongs to reason, as I have said before.[8] But there is only one power of reason in human beings. Therefore, there is only one precept of the natural law.

On the contrary, the precepts of the natural law in human beings are related to action as the first principles in scientific matters are related to theoretical knowledge. But there are several indemonstrable first principles of theoretical knowledge. Therefore, there are also several precepts of the natural law.

I answer that, as I have said before,[9] the precepts of the natural law are related to practical reason as the first principles of scientific demonstrations are related to theoretical reason. For both the precepts of the natural law and the first principles of scientific demonstrations are self-evident principles. And we speak of things being self-evident in two ways: in one way as such; in a second way in relation to ourselves. We indeed speak of self-evident propositions as such when their predicates belong to the nature of their subjects, although such propositions may not be self-evident to those who do not know the definition of the subjects. For example, the proposition "Human beings are rational" is by its nature self-evident, since to speak of something human is to speak of something rational, although the proposition is not self-evident to one who does not know what a human being is. And so, as Boethius says in his work *On Groups of Seven,*[10] there are axioms or universally self-evident propositions, and propositions whose terms all persons know (e.g., "Every whole is greater than one of its parts" and "Things equal to the same thing are themselves equal") are such. But some propositions are self-evident only to the wise, who understand what the proposition's terms signify. For example, for those who understand that angels are not material substances, it is self-evident that angels are not circumscriptively in a place, something not evident to the uneducated, who do not understand the nature of angels.

And there is a priority regarding the things that fall within the understanding of all persons. For what first falls within our understanding is being, the understanding of which is included in everything that one understands. And so the first indemonstrable principle is that one cannot at the same time affirm and deny the same thing. And this principle is based on the nature of being and nonbeing, and all other principles are based on it, as the *Metaphysics* says.[11] And as being is the first thing that without qualification falls within our understanding, so good is the first thing that falls within the understanding of practical reason. And practi-

---

[8] I–II, Q. 90, A. 1.   [9] I–II, Q. 91, A. 3.   [10] *On Groups of Seven* (PL 64:1311). This work is otherwise known as *How Substances as Existing Things Are Good.*   [11] Aristotle, *Metaphysics* III, 3 (1005b29–34).

cal reason is ordered to action, since every efficient cause acts for the sake of an end, which has the nature of good. And so the first principle in practical reason is one based on the nature of good, namely, that good is what all things seek. Therefore, the first precept of the natural law is that we should do and seek good, and shun evil. And all the other precepts of the natural law are based on that precept, namely, that all the things that practical reason by nature understands to be human goods or evils belong to precepts of the natural law as things to be done or shunned.

And since good has the nature of end, and evil the nature of the contrary, reason by nature understands to be good all the things for which human beings have a natural inclination, and so to be things to be actively sought, and understands contrary things as evil and to be shunned. Therefore, the ordination of our natural inclinations ordains the precepts of the natural law.

First, for example, human beings have an inclination for good by the nature they share with all substances, namely, as every substance by nature seeks to preserve itself. And regarding this inclination, means that preserve our human life and prevent the contrary belong to the natural law.

Second, human beings have more particular inclinations by the nature they share with other animals. And so the *Digest* says that things "that nature has taught all animals," such as the sexual union of male and female, and the upbringing of children, and the like, belong to the natural law.[12]

Third, human beings have inclinations for good by their rational nature, which is proper to them. For example, human beings by nature have inclinations to know truths about God and to live in society with other human beings. And so things that relate to such inclinations belong to the natural law (e.g., that human beings shun ignorance, that they not offend those with whom they ought to live sociably, and other such things regarding those inclinations).

Reply Obj. 1. All the precepts of the natural law, insofar as they relate to one first precept, have the nature of one natural law.

Reply Obj. 2. All the inclinations of any part of human nature (e.g., the concupiscible and irascible powers), insofar as reason rules them, belong to the natural law and are traced to one first precept, as I have said.[13] And so there are many precepts of the natural law as such, but they share a common foundation.

---

[12] Justinian, *Digest* I, title 1, law 1.   [13] In the body of the article.

Reply Obj. 3. Reason, although as such one power, ordains everything that concerns human beings. And so the law of reason includes everything that reason can rule.

THIRD ARTICLE
Do All Virtuous Acts Belong to the Natural Law?

We proceed thus to the third inquiry. It seems that not all virtuous acts belong to the natural law, for the following reasons:

Objection 1. It belongs to the nature of law that law be ordained for the common good, as I have said before.[14] But some virtuous acts are ordained for the private good of an individual, as is particularly evident in the case of acts of the virtue of moderation. Therefore, not all virtuous acts are subject to the natural law.

Obj. 2. All sins are contrary to certain virtuous acts. Therefore, if all virtuous acts belong to the natural law, it seems that all sins are consequently contrary to nature. And yet we say this in a special way about some sins.

Obj. 3. Everybody agrees about things that are in accord with nature. But not everybody agrees about virtuous acts, for things that are virtuous for some are vicious for others. Therefore, not all virtuous acts belong to the natural law.

On the contrary, Damascene says in his work *On Orthodox Faith* that "virtues are natural."[15] Therefore, virtuous acts are also subject to the natural law.

I answer that we can speak about virtuous acts in two ways: in one way as virtuous; in a second way as we consider such acts in their own species. Therefore, if we are speaking about virtuous acts as virtuous, then all virtuous acts belong to the natural law. For I have said that everything to which human beings are inclined by their nature belongs to the natural law.[16] But everything is by its nature inclined to the activity that its form renders fitting. For example, fire is inclined to heat things. And so, since the rational soul is the specific form of human beings, everyone has an inclination from one's nature to act in accord with reason. And this is to act virtuously. And so in this regard, all virtuous acts belong to the natural law, since one's own reason by nature dictates that one act virtuously.

But if we should be speaking about virtuous acts as such and such, namely, as we consider them in their own species, then not all virtuous acts belong to the natural law. For we do many things virtuously to which

---

[14] I–II, Q. 90, A. 2.   [15] *On Orthodox Faith* III, 14 (PG 94:1045).   [16] A. 2.

nature does not at first incline us, but which human beings by the inquiry of reason have discovered to be useful for living righteously.

Reply Obj. 1. Moderation concerns the natural desires for food and drink and sex, which desires are indeed ordained for the natural common good, just as other prescriptions of the natural law are ordained for the common moral good.

Reply Obj. 2. We can call the nature proper to human beings the nature of human beings. And so all sins, insofar as they are contrary to reason, are also contrary to nature, as Damascene makes clear in his work *On Orthodox Faith*.[17] Or else we can call the nature common to human beings and other animals the nature of human beings. And so we speak of certain particular sins being contrary to nature. For example, the sexual intercourse of males, which we specifically call the sin contrary to nature, is contrary to the sexual union of male and female, and such sexual union is natural for all animals.

Reply Obj. 3. The argument of this objection is valid regarding virtuous acts as such and such. For then, because of the different conditions of human beings, some acts may be virtuous for some persons, as proportionate and suitable for them, which are nonetheless wicked for other persons, as disproportionate for them.

FOURTH ARTICLE
Is the Natural Law the Same for All Human Beings?

We thus proceed to the fourth inquiry. It seems that the natural law is not the same for all human beings, for the following reasons:

Objection 1. The *Decretum* says that "the natural law is contained in the [Old] Law and the Gospel."[18] But what is contained in the Law and the Gospel is not in the common possession of all, since Rom. 10:16 says: "Some do not heed the Gospel." Therefore, the natural law is not the same for all human beings.

Obj. 2. "We call things in accord with law just," as the *Ethics* says.[19] But the same work says that nothing is so universally just that it is not otherwise for some.[20] Therefore, even the natural law is not the same for all human beings.

Obj. 3. Things to which human beings' nature inclines them belong to the natural law, as I have said before.[21] But nature inclines different human beings to different things. For example, nature inclines some to

---

[17]*On Orthodox Faith* II, 4 and 30 (PG 94:876, 976).   [18]Gratian, *Decretum* I, dist. 1, preface.   [19]Aristotle, *Ethics* V, 1 (1129b12).   [20]Ibid. V, 7 (1134b32).   [21]AA. 2, 3.

desire pleasures, others to desire honors, others to desire other things. Therefore, the natural law is not the same for all human beings.

On the contrary, Isidore says in his *Etymologies:* "The natural law is common to all nations."[22]

I answer that things to which nature inclines human beings belong to the natural law, as I have said before,[23] and one of the things proper to human beings is that their nature inclines them to act in accord with reason. And it belongs to reason to advance from the general to the particular, as the *Physics* makes clear.[24] And regarding that process, theoretical reason proceeds in one way, and practical reason in another way. For inasmuch as theoretical reason is especially concerned about necessary things, which cannot be otherwise disposed, its particular conclusions, just like its general principles, are true without exception. But practical reason is concerned about contingent things, which include human actions. And so the more reason goes from the general to the particular, the more exceptions we find, although there is some necessity in the general principles. Therefore, truth in theoretical matters, both first principles and conclusions, is the same for all human beings, although some know only the truth of the principles, which we call universal propositions, and not the truth of the conclusions. But truth in practical matters, or practical rectitude, is the same for all human beings only regarding the general principles, not regarding the particular conclusions. And not all of those with practical rectitude regarding particulars know the truth in equal measure.

Therefore, the truth or rectitude regarding the general principles of both theoretical and practical reason is the same for all persons and known in equal measure by all of them. And the truth regarding the particular conclusions of theoretical reason is the same for all persons, but some know such truth less than others. For example, it is true for all persons that triangles have three angles equal to two right angles, although not everybody knows this.

But the truth or rectitude regarding particular conclusions of practical reason is neither the same for all persons nor known in equal measure even by those for whom it is the same. For example, it is correct and true for all persons that they should act in accord with reason. And it follows as a particular conclusion from this principle that those holding goods in trust should return the goods to the goods' owners. And this is indeed true for the most part, but it might in particular cases be injurious, and so

---

[22] *Etymologies* V, 4 (PL 82:199).   [23] AA. 2, 3.   [24] Aristotle, *Physics* I, 1 (184a16–27).

contrary to reason, to return the goods (e.g., if the owner should be seeking to attack one's country). And the more the particular conclusion goes into particulars, the more exceptions there are (e.g., if one should declare that entrusted goods should be returned to their owners with such and such safeguards or in such and such ways). For the more particular conditions are added to the particular conclusion, the more ways there may be exceptions, so that the conclusion about returning or not returning entrusted goods is erroneous.

Therefore, we should say that the natural law regarding general first principles is the same for all persons both as to their rectitude and as to knowledge of them. And the natural law regarding particulars, which are, as it were, conclusions from the general principles, is for the most part the same for all persons both as to its rectitude and as to knowledge of it. Nonetheless, it can be wanting in rather few cases both as to its rectitude and as to knowledge of it. As to rectitude, the natural law can be wanting because of particular obstacles, just as natures that come to be and pass away are wanting in rather few cases because of obstacles. And also as to knowledge of the natural law, the law can be wanting because emotions or evil habituation or evil natural disposition has perverted the reason of some. For example, the Germans of old did not consider robbery wicked, as Caesar's *Gallic Wars* relates,[25] although robbery is expressly contrary to the natural law.

Reply Obj. 1. We should not understand the cited statement to mean that all the matters included in the Law and the Gospel belong to the natural law, since the Law and the Gospel transmit to us many things above nature. Rather, we should understand the statement to mean that the Law and the Gospel completely transmit to us the things that belong to the natural law. And so Gratian, after saying that "the natural law is contained in the Law and the Gospel," immediately adds by way of example: "And everyone is thereby commanded to do unto others what one wishes to be done to oneself."

Reply Obj. 2. We should understand the cited statement of the Philosopher regarding things just by nature as conclusions derived from general principles, not as the general principles. And such conclusions are correct for the most part and are wanting in rather few cases.

Reply Obj. 3. As the power of reason in human beings rules and commands other powers, so reason needs to direct all the natural inclinations belonging to other powers. And so it is universally correct for all persons to direct all their inclinations by reason.

---

[25] Julius Caesar, *Gallic Wars* VI, 23.

FIFTH ARTICLE
Can the Natural Law Vary?

We thus proceed to the fifth inquiry. It seems that the natural law can vary, for the following reasons:

Objection 1. A gloss on Sir. 17:9, "He [God] supplied them with instruction and the law of life," says: "He wanted the [Old] Law to be written in order to correct the natural law."[26] But what is corrected is changed. Therefore, the natural law can vary.

Obj. 2. The killing of innocent human beings as well as adultery and theft are contrary to the natural law. But God altered these precepts. For example, God on one occasion commanded Abraham to slay his innocent son, as Gen. 22:2 relates. And God on another occasion commanded the Jews to steal vessels the Egyptians had lent them, as Ex. 12:35–36 relates. And God on another occasion commanded Hosea to take a fornicating wife, as Hos. 1:2 relates. Therefore, the natural law can vary.

Obj. 3. Isidore says in his *Etymologies* that "the common possession of all property and the same freedom for all persons belong to the natural law."[27] But we perceive that human laws have altered these prescriptions. Therefore, it seems that the natural law can vary.

On the contrary, the *Decretum* says: "The natural law originates with rational creatures. It does not vary over time and abides without change."[28]

I answer that we can understand the mutability of the natural law in two ways. We can understand it in one way by things being added to it. And then nothing prevents the natural law changing, since both divine law and human laws add to natural law many things beneficial to human life.

We can understand the mutability of the natural law in a second way by way of substraction, namely, that things previously subject to the law cease to be so. And then the natural law is altogether immutable as to its first principles. And as to its secondary precepts, which we said are proper proximate conclusions, as it were, from the first principles,[29] the natural law is not so changed that what it prescribes is not for the most part completely correct. But it can be changed regarding particulars and in rather few cases, due to special causes that prevent observance of such precepts, as I have said before.[30]

Reply Obj. 1. We say that written law has been given to correct the natural law either because the written law supplements what the natural law lacked, or because the natural law in the hearts of some regarding

---

[26] *Glossa ordinaria*, on Sir. 17:9 (PL 109:876; 113:1201).   [27] *Etymologies* V, 4 (PL 82:199).   [28] Gratian, *Decretum* I, dist. 5, preface.   [29] A. 4.   [30] Ibid.

particulars had been corrupted insofar as they thought that things by nature evil were good. And such corruption needed correction.

Reply Obj. 2. All human beings, without exception, both the innocent and the guilty, die when natural death comes. And God's power indeed inflicts such natural death on human beings because of original sin, as 1 Sam. 2:6 says: "The Lord causes death and life." And so, at the command of God, death can without any injustice be inflicted on any human being, whether guilty or innocent.

Likewise, adultery is sexual intercourse with another man's wife, whom the law handed down by God has allotted to him. And so there is no adultery or fornication in having intercourse with any woman at the command of God.

And the argument is the same regarding theft, which consists of taking another's property. One does not take without the consent of the owner (i.e., steal) anything that one takes at the command of God, who is the owner of all property.

Nor is it only regarding human affairs that everything God commands is owed to him. Rather, regarding things of nature, everything God does is also in one respect natural, as I said in the First Part.[31]

Reply Obj. 3. We speak of things belonging to the natural law in two ways. We speak of them belonging in one way because nature inclines us to them. For example, one should not cause injury to another. We speak of them belonging in a second way because nature did not introduce the contrary. For example, we could say that it belongs to the natural law that human beings are naked, since nature did not endow them with clothes, which human skill created. And it is in the latter way that we say that "the common possession of all property and the same freedom for all persons" belong to the natural law, namely, that the reason of human beings, not nature, introduced private property and compulsory servitude. And so the natural law in this respect varies only by way of addition.

SIXTH ARTICLE

Can the Natural Law Be Excised from the Hearts of Human Beings?

We thus proceed to the sixth inquiry. It seems that the natural law can be excised from the hearts of human beings, for the following reasons:

Objection 1. A gloss on Rom. 2:14, "When the Gentiles, who do not have the law," etc., says: "The law of righteousness, which sin had wiped

---

[31] I, Q. 105, A. 6, *ad* 1.

out, is inscribed on the inner human being renewed by grace."[32] But the law of righteousness is the natural law. Therefore, the natural law can be wiped out.

Obj. 2. The law of grace is more efficacious than the law of nature. But sin destroys the law of grace. Therefore, much more can the natural law be wiped out.

Obj. 3. What law establishes is rendered just, as it were. But human beings have established many things contrary to the natural law. Therefore, the natural law can be excised from the hearts of human beings.

On the contrary, Augustine says in his *Confessions:* "Your law is inscribed on the hearts of human beings, and indeed no wickedness wipes it out."[33] But the law inscribed on the hearts of human beings is the natural law. Therefore, the natural law cannot be wiped out.

I answer that, as I have said before,[34] there belong to the natural law, indeed primarily, very general precepts, precepts that everyone knows, and more particular, secondary precepts, which are like proximate conclusions from first principles. Therefore, regarding the general principles, the natural law in general can in no way be excised from the hearts of human beings. But the natural law is wiped out regarding particular actions insofar as desires or other emotions prevent reason from applying the general principles to particular actions, as I have said before.[35]

And the natural law can be excised from the hearts of human beings regarding the other, secondary precepts, either because of wicked opinions, just as errors in theoretical matters happen regarding necessary conclusions, or because of evil customs or corrupt habits. For example, some did not think robbery a sin, or even sins against nature to be sinful, as the Apostle also says in Rom. 1:24–28.

Reply Obj. 1. Sin wipes out the natural law regarding particulars but not in general, except perhaps regarding secondary precepts of the natural law, in the way I mentioned.[36]

Reply Obj. 2. Although grace is more efficacious than nature, nature is nonetheless more essential to human beings and so more abiding.

Reply Obj. 3. The argument of this objection is valid regarding the secondary precepts of the natural law, contrary to which some lawmakers have passed wicked statutes.

---

[32]*Glossa ordinaria,* on Rom. 2:14 (PL 114:476); Peter Lombard, *Glossa,* on Rom. 2:14 (PL 191:1345).　　[33]*Confessions* II, 4 (PL 32:678).　　[34]AA. 4, 5.　　[35]I–II, Q. 77, A. 2.　　[36]In the body of the article.

QUESTION 95

On Human Law

FIRST ARTICLE
Was It Beneficial That Human Beings Establish Laws?

We thus proceed to the first inquiry. It seems that it was not beneficial that human beings establish laws, for the following reasons:

Objection 1. The purpose of every law is to make human beings good, as I have said before.[1] But admonitions induce human beings willingly to live rightly more than laws do coercively. Therefore, there was no need to establish laws.

Obj. 2. The Philosopher says in the *Ethics:* "Human beings have recourse to judges as justice-in-the-flesh."[2] But justice-in-the-flesh is better than the inanimate justice contained in laws. Therefore, it would have been better to commit the execution of justice to the decisions of judges than to establish laws to supplement their decisions.

Obj. 3. Every law directs human actions, as is evident from what I have said before.[3] But since human acts regard particular things, which are potentially infinite, no one except wise persons, who regard particulars, can sufficiently contemplate the things that belong to the direction of human acts. Therefore, it would have been better that the decisions of wise persons direct human actions than that any established law should. Therefore, there was no need to establish human laws.

On the contrary, Isidore says in his *Etymologies:* "Laws were established so that fear of them curb human audacity, and that innocence be safe in the midst of the wicked, and that the fear of punishment restrain the ability of the wicked to inflict harm."[4] But the human race most needs such things. Therefore, it was necessary to establish human laws.

I answer that, as is evident from what I have said before,[5] human beings by nature have a capacity for virtue, but they need to arrive at the very perfection of virtue by some training.[6] Just so, we perceive that industriousness

---

[1] I–II, Q. 92, A. 1.   [1] *Ethics* V, 4 (1132a22).   [3] I–II, Q. 90, AA. 1, 2.
[4] *Etymologies* V, 20 (PL 82:202).   [5] I–II: Q. 63, A. 1; Q. 94, A. 3.   [6] Thomas Aquinas generally uses the Latin word "*disciplina*" to mean "instruction." But the instruction at issue here and elsewhere in reference to human law is practical and formative, with coercion the punishment for noncompliance. I accordingly translate "*disciplina*" in this context as "training."

helps them regarding their necessities (e.g., food and clothing). And nature gives them the sources to provide these necessities, namely, reason and hands, not the full complement of the necessities that nature gives other animals, for whom nature has sufficiently provided covering and food.

But human beings are not readily self-sufficient in regard to this training, since the perfection of virtue consists chiefly of human beings' restraint from excessive pleasures, toward which they are most prone. And this is especially true of youths, for whom training is more efficacious. And so human beings receive such training, whereby they arrive at virtue, from others. And indeed regarding youths prone to virtuous acts by good natural disposition or habituation (or, rather, a gift from God), paternal training, which consists of admonitions, suffices.

But some persons are wicked and prone to vices, and cannot be easily persuaded by words. Therefore, force and fear were needed to restrain them from evil. Consequently, at least desisting from evil deeds, they would both leave others in peace and be themselves at length brought by such habituation to do voluntarily what they hitherto did out of fear, and so become virtuous. But such training, which compels by fear of punishment, is the training administered by laws. And so it was necessary to establish laws in order that human beings live in peace and have virtue. For, as the Philosopher says in the *Politics:* "As human beings, if perfect in virtue, are the best of animals, so are they, if cut off from law and justice, the worst of all animals."[7] This is because human beings, unlike other animals, have the tools of reason to satisfy their disordered desires and beastly rages.

Reply Obj. 1. Voluntary admonitions induce well disposed human beings to virtue better than compulsion does, but there are some who are not induced to virtue unless they be compelled.

Reply Obj. 2. The Philosopher says in the *Rhetoric:* "It is better that law direct all things than that they be left to the decisions of judges."[8] And this is so for three reasons. First, indeed, it is easier to find the few wise persons sufficient to establish right laws than the many wise persons necessary to judge rightly about particular matters. Second, lawmakers consider over a long time what to impose by law, but judges reach decisions about particular deeds as cases spontaneously arise. And human beings can more easily perceive what is right by considering many instances than they can by considering only one deed. Third, lawmakers decide in general and about future events, but presiding judges decide current cases, and love or hatred or covetousness affects such decisions. And so their decisions are perverted.

---

[7] *Politics* I, 1 (1253a31–33). [8] *Rhetoric* I, 1 (1354a31–34).

Therefore, since few embody the justice required of a judge, and since that justice can be perverted, it was necessary that law determine, whenever possible, what judges should decide, and commit very few matters to the decisions of human beings.

Reply Obj. 3. "We need to commit to judges" certain particular details, which laws cannot encompass, as the Philosopher also says in the *Rhetoric*,[9] such as, "whether alleged deeds have or have not been done," and the like.

SECOND ARTICLE
Is Every Human Law Derived from the Natural Law?

We thus proceed to the second inquiry. It seems that not every human law is derived from the natural law, for the following reasons:

Objection 1. The Philosopher says in the *Ethics* that "it does not at all matter originally whether one effects legal justice in this or that way."[10] But regarding obligations to which the natural law gives rise, it does matter whether one effects justice in this or that way. Therefore, not all the things established by human laws are derived from the natural law.

Obj. 2. Positive law differs from natural law, as Isidore makes clear in his *Etymologies*[11] and the Philosopher makes clear in the *Ethics*.[12] But things derived as conclusions from the general principles of the natural law belong to the natural law, as I have said before.[13] Therefore, things proper to human law are not derived from the natural law.

Obj. 3. The natural law is the same for all persons. For the Philosopher says in the *Ethics* that "natural justice has the same force everywhere."[14] Therefore, if human laws were to be derived from the natural law, human laws would likewise be the same for all persons. But such a conclusion is evidently false.

Obj. 4. We can assign reasons for things derived from the natural law. But "one cannot assign reasons for all the statutes rulers have decreed," as the Jurist says.[15] Therefore, some human laws are not derived from the natural law.

On the contrary, Cicero says in his *Rhetoric:* "Fear and reverence for the laws have prescribed things derived from nature and approved by custom."[16]

I answer that Augustine says in his work *On Free Choice:* "Unjust laws do not seem to be laws."[17] And so laws have binding force insofar as they

---

[9]Ibid. I, 1 (1354b13).   [10]*Ethics* V, 7 (1134b20).   [11]*Etymologies* V, 4 (PL 82:199).   [12]*Ethics* V, 7 (1134b18–19).   [13]I–II, Q. 94, A. 4.   [14]*Ethics* V, 7 (1134b19–20).   [15]*Digest* I, title 3, law 20.   [16]*Rhetoric* II, 53.   [17]*On Free Choice* I, 5, n. 11 (PL 32:1227).

have justice. And we say regarding human affairs that things are just because they are right according to the rule of reason. But the primary rule of reason is the natural law, as is evident from what I have said before.[18] And so every human law has as much of the nature of law as it is derived from the natural law. And a human law diverging in any way from the natural law will be a perversion of law and no longer a law.

But we should note that we can derive things from the natural law in two ways: in one way as conclusions from its first principles; in a second way as specifications of certain general principles. Indeed, the first way is like the way in which we draw conclusions from first principles in theoretical sciences. And the second way is like the way that craftsmen in the course of exercising their skill adapt general forms to specific things. For example, a builder needs to adapt the general form of a house to this or that shape of a house. Therefore, some things are derived from general principles of the natural law as conclusions. For example, one can derive the prohibition against homicide from the general principle that one should do no evil to anyone. And some things are derived from general principles of the natural law as specifications. For example, the natural law ordains that criminals should be punished, but that criminals be punished in this or that way is a specification of the natural law.

Therefore, human laws are derived from the natural law in both ways. Things derived from the natural law in the first way are not only contained in human laws as established by those laws, but they also have part of their binding force from the natural law. But things derived from the natural law in the second way have all of their binding force from human law.

Reply Obj. 1. The Philosopher is speaking about the things laws decreed by determining or specifying one of the precepts of the natural law.

Reply Obj. 2. The argument of this objection is valid regarding things derived from the natural law as conclusions.

Reply Obj. 3. The general principles of the natural law cannot be applied to all peoples in the same way because of the great variety of human affairs. And so there are different positive laws for different peoples.

Reply Obj. 4. We should understand the Jurist's statement to regard things decreed by rulers about particular specifications of the natural law. And the judgments of experienced and prudent persons are indeed related to such specifications as certain principles underlying their judgments, namely, inasmuch as they immediately perceive what is the most fitting particular specification. And so the Philosopher says in the *Ethics* that "we should" in such matters "attend to the intuitive statements and

---

[18]I–II, Q. 91, A. 2, *ad* 2.

opinions of the experienced and the mature or prudent no less than to their arguments."[19]

THIRD ARTICLE
Does Isidore Appropriately Describe
the Characteristics of Positive Law?

We thus proceed to the third inquiry. Isidore says: "Laws should be virtuous, just, possible by nature, in accord with a country's customs, suitable to time and place, necessary, useful, so clear that they contain nothing obscure to cause deception, and decreed for the common benefit of all citizens, not the private benefit of some."[20] It seems that he in this way inappropriately describes the characteristics of positive law, for the following reasons:

Objection 1. Isidore previously had explained the characteristics of law in terms of three conditions: "Laws should be everything constituted by reason if befitting religion, suitable for training, and useful for the commonweal."[21] Therefore, he later unnecessarily added further conditions of law.

Obj. 2. Justice is a virtue, as Cicero says in his work *On Duties*.[22] Therefore, Isidore needlessly adds "just" after he mentioned "virtuous."

Obj. 3. Isidore contradistinguished written laws from customs.[23] Therefore, he ought not to have posited in the definition of law that laws be "in accord with a country's customs."

Obj. 4. We call things necessary in two ways. Things that cannot be otherwise, are absolutely necessary, and such necessary things are not subject to human judgment. And so such necessity does not belong to human law. Other things are necessary for ends, and such necessity is the same as usefulness. Therefore, Isidore needlessly posits both "necessary" and "useful" as characteristics of law.

On the contrary, there stands the authority of Isidore himself.

I answer that we need to determine the form of any means in relation to the end desired. For example, the form of a saw is such as to be suitable for cutting wood, as the *Physics* makes clear.[24] Likewise, everything ruled and measured needs to have a form apportioned to its rule or measure. And human law has both, since it is both something ordained for an end and a rule or measure ruled or measured by a higher measure. And the higher measure is indeed of two kinds, namely, the divine law and the natural law, as is evident from what I have said before.[25] But the end of human law is

---

[19] *Ethics* VI, 11 (1143b11–13).   [20] *Etymologies* V, 21 (PL 82:203).   [21] Ibid. V, 3 (PL 82:199).   [22] *On Duties* I, 7.   [23] *Etymologies* II, 10 (PL 82:131); V, 3 (PL 82:199).   [24] Aristotle, *Physics* II, 9 (200a10–13, b5–9).   [25] A. 1; I–II, Q. 93, A. 3.

the benefit of human beings, as the Jurist also says.[26] And so indeed Isidore first posited three things as conditions of human law, namely, that human law benefit religion (i.e., as human law is properly related to the divine law), that human law be suitable for training (i.e., as human law is properly related to the natural law), that human law be useful for the commonweal (i.e., as human law is properly related to human usefulness).

And all the other conditions that he later mentions are traceable to these three things. For what he calls virtuous is a reference to what befits religion. And by adding that human laws be "just, possible by nature, in accord with a country's customs, suitable to the place and time," he indicates that the laws should be suitable for training. For we indeed first consider human training in relation to the ordination of reason, which ordination is implied in what he calls just. Second, we consider human training in relation to the capacity of human agents. For training ought to be suitable to each according to the capacity of each, including natural capacity. (For example, one should not impose the same training on children that one imposes on adults.) And training ought to be suitable according to human customs, since human beings do not live in society by themselves, not manifesting their behavior to others. Third, in relation to requisite circumstances, he says: "suitable to the place and time."

And the additional words, "necessary," "useful," and so forth, refer to what facilitates the commonweal. For example, necessity refers to removing evils, usefulness to acquiring benefits, and clarification to preventing harm that could arise from the laws themselves.

And he indicates that human laws are ordained for the common good, as I have previously affirmed,[27] in the last part of the definition.

Reply Objs. 1–4. The answer makes clear the replies to the objections.

FOURTH ARTICLE
Does Isidore Appropriately Designate Kinds of Human Law?[28]

We thus proceed to the fourth inquiry. It seems that Isidore does not appropriately designate kinds of human law, for the following reasons:

Objection 1. Isidore includes in human law "the common law of peoples," which he so names, as he says, because "almost every people possesses it."[29] But "natural law is common to all peoples," as he himself says.[30] Therefore, the common law of peoples is contained in the natural law rather than positive human law.

---

[26]*Digest* I, title 3, law 25.   [27]I–II, Q. 90, A. 2.   [28]*Etymologies* V, 4 (PL 82: 199ff).   [29]Ibid. V, 6 (PL 82:200).   [30]Ibid. V, 4 (PL 82:199).

Obj. 2. Things that have the same binding force seem to differ only materially, not formally. But "statutes, plebiscites, decrees of the senate," and the other like things Isidore describes[31] all have the same binding force. Therefore, they seem to differ only materially. But artisans should pay no attention to such differences, since there can be an endless number of them. Therefore, Isidore inappropriately introduces such divisions.

Obj. 3. As there are rulers and priests and soldiers in political communities, so human beings also have other public duties. Therefore, as Isidore posits "military law" and "public law" (which govern priests and magistrates),[32] so he should also posit other laws pertaining to other public duties.

Obj. 4. We should ignore accidental things. But it is accidental to laws whether they are framed by this or that human being. Therefore, Isidore inappropriately posits a division of laws by the names of their framers,[33] namely, that one is called the Cornelian law, another the Falcidian law, and so forth.

On the contrary, the authority of Isidore suffices.

I answer that we can intrinsically distinguish each thing by what belongs to its nature. For example, the nature of animals includes a soul that is rational or nonrational. And so we properly and intrinsically distinguish animals by whether they are rational or irrational, and not by whether they are black or white, which are characteristics altogether outside the nature of animals.

And many characteristics belong to the nature of human laws, and we can properly and intrinsically distinguish human laws by any of those things. For example, it first of all belongs to the nature of human laws that they be derived from the natural law, as is evident from what I have said before.[34] And we in this respect divide positive laws into the common law of peoples and the laws of particular commonwealths by the two ways in which things may be derived from the natural law, as I have said before.[35] For precepts derived from the natural law as conclusions from its general principles belong to the common law of peoples (e.g., just buying and selling, and the like, without which human beings cannot live sociably with one another). And living sociably with others belongs to the natural law, since human beings are by nature social animals, as the *Politics* proves.[36] But precepts derived from the natural law by way of particular specifications belong to the laws of particular commonwealths, whereby each commonwealth specifies things suitable for itself.

Second, it belongs to the nature of human laws that they be ordained for the common good of a political community. And we can in this respect

---

[31] Ibid. V, 9 (PL 82:200).   [32] Ibid. V, 7 and 8 (PL 82:200).   [33] Ibid. V, 15 (PL 82:201).   [34] A. 2.   [35] Ibid.   [36] Aristotle, *Politics* I, 1 (1253a2–3).

distinguish human laws by the different kinds of persons who perform particular tasks for the common good (e.g., priests, who pray to God for the people; rulers, who govern the people; soldiers, who fight for the safety of the people). And so special laws are adapted for such persons.

Third, it belongs to the nature of human laws that they be established by those who govern the political community, as I have said before.[37] And we in this respect distinguish human laws by the different forms of governing political communities. And as the Philosopher says in the *Politics*,[38] one of these forms is monarchy (i.e., rule by one person). And we understand the laws of monarchical regimes as royal decrees. And aristocracy (i.e., rule by the best persons or aristocrats) is another form of government. And we understand the laws of aristocratic regimes as the authoritative legal opinions of the wise, and also as the decrees of the senate. And oligarchy (i.e., rule by a few rich and powerful persons) is another form of government. And we understand the laws of oligarchical regimes as magisterial law, also called law by dignitaries. And another form of government is by the people, which form we call democracy. And we understand the laws of democratic regimes as laws by the people. (Tyranny is another form of government, an altogether corrupt form, and so we do not understand the laws of tyrannical regimes as any law.) There is also a form of government that is a mixture of the good forms, and this mixed form of government is the best. And we understand the laws of such regimes as law "prescribed by elders and the people," as Isidore says.[39]

Fourth, it belongs to the nature of human laws that they direct human actions. And we in this respect distinguish laws, which we sometimes designate by their authors, by the laws' different subject matter. For example, we distinguish the Julian Law on adultery,[40] the Cornelian Law on assassination,[41] and the like, because of their subject matter, not because of their authors.

Reply Obj. 1. The common law of peoples is indeed natural for human beings in one respect, insofar as it is rational, since it is derived from the natural law as conclusions not very remote from general principles of the natural law. And so human beings easily agree about such matters. But we distinguish the common law of peoples from the natural law, especially from what is common to all animals.

Reply Objs. 2–4. The replies to these objections is evident from what I have said.[42]

---

[37] I–II, Q. 90, A. 3.   [38] *Politics* III, 7 (1279a23–b10).   [39] *Etymologies* II, 10 (PL 82:130); V, 10 (PL 82:200).   [40] Justinian, *Digest* XLVIII, title 5.   [41] Ibid. XLVIII, title 8.   [42] In the body of the article.

QUESTION 96

On the Power of Human Laws

FIRST ARTICLE
Should Human Laws Be Framed in Particular
Rather Than General Terms?

We thus proceed to the first inquiry. It seems that human laws should be framed in particular rather than general terms, for the following reasons:

Objection 1. The Philosopher says in the *Ethics* that "things of the legal order consist of everything laws decree about individual matters, and likewise of judicial decisions,"[1] which also concern particular matters, since judges hand down decisions on particular cases. Therefore, laws are framed both in general and in particular terms.

Obj. 2. Laws direct human actions, as I have said before.[2] But human actions consist of particular things. Therefore, laws should be framed in particular rather than general terms.

Obj. 3. Laws are the rules and measures of human actions, as I have said before.[3] But measures should be most certain, as the *Metaphysics* says.[4] Therefore, since nothing about human actions can be so universally certain as not to be wanting in particular cases, it seems that laws need to be framed in particular rather than general terms.

On the contrary, the Jurist says: "Laws need to be framed to suit things that more frequently happen, and laws are not framed to suit things that can happen once in a while."[5]

I answer that everything for an end needs to be proportioned to the end. But the end of law is the common good, since "laws should be framed for the common benefit of citizens, not for any private benefit," as Isidore says in his *Etymologies*.[6] And so human laws need to be proportioned to the common good. But the common good consists of many things. And so laws need to regard many things, both persons, matters, and times. For the political community consists of many persons, and its good is procured by many actions. Nor is it instituted to endure only for a short time but to last for all time through successive generations of citizens, as Augustine says in *The City of God*.[7]

---

[1] *Ethics* V, 7 (1134b23–24).   [2] I–II, Q. 90, AA. 1, 2.   [3] Ibid.   [4] *Metaphysics* X, 1 (1053a1–8).   [5] *Digest* I, title 3, laws 3, 4.   [6] *Etymologies* II, 10 (PL 82:131); V, 21 (PL 82:203).   [7] *The City of God* XXII, 6 (PL 41:759).

Reply Obj. 1. The Philosopher in the *Ethics* posits three parts of legal justice (i.e., positive law).[8] For there are certain prescriptions framed only in general terms, and these are general laws. And regarding such laws, he says that "legal justice indeed does not originally differentiate in particulars but does once established."[9] For example, captives are ransomed at a fixed price.

And there are some laws that are general in one respect and particular in another. And we call such laws privileges, that is, private laws, since they regard particular persons, and yet the power of these laws extends to many matters. And it is regarding these that the Philosopher adds: "And, further, everything laws decree in particular cases."[10]

And we call some things legal because general laws are applied to particular cases, not because the applications are laws. For example, judges hand down decisions that we consider legally binding. And it is regarding such that the Philosopher adds: "And judicial decisions."[11]

Reply Obj. 2. Something directive needs to direct several things, and so the Philosopher says in the *Metaphysics* that all the things belonging to a genus are measured by the one of them that primarily belongs to the genus.[12] For if there were to be as many rules or measures as things measured or ruled, a rule or measure, which is that one thing enable many things to be known, would cease to be of any use. And so a law would have no usefulness if it were to cover only a single action. For wise persons give individual commands to direct individual actions, but law is a general command, as I have said.[13]

Reply Obj. 3. "One should not look for the same certainty in all kinds of things," as the *Ethics* says.[14] And so in the case of contingent things like natural events and human affairs, there is sufficient certainty if things are true for the most part, even though they sometimes fail to happen in relatively few cases.

SECOND ARTICLE
Does It Belong to Human Laws to Prohibit All Vices?

We thus proceed to the second inquiry. It seems that it belongs to human laws to prohibit all vices, for the following reasons:

Objection 1. Isidore says in his *Etymologies* that "laws have been established in order to curb human audacity out of fear of them."[15] But human

---

[8]*Ethics* V, 7 (1134b20–24).   [9]Ibid. V, 7 (1134b20–21).   [10]Ibid. V, 7 (1134b23).
[11]Ibid. V, 7 (1134b24).   [12]*Metaphysics* X, 1 (1052b18–22).   [13]I–II, Q. 92, A.
2, obj. 1 (citing Justinian).   [14]Aristotle, *Ethics* I, 3 (1094b13–22).   [15]*Etymologies* V, 20 (PL 82:202).

audacity would not be sufficiently curbed unless laws were to prohibit everything evil. Therefore, human laws ought to prohibit everything evil.

Obj. 2. The aim of lawmakers is to make citizens virtuous. But citizens can be virtuous only if they are curbed of all vices. Therefore, it belongs to human law to curb all vices.

Obj. 3. Human law is derived from natural law, as I have said before.[16] But all sins are contrary to the natural law. Therefore, human law ought to prohibit all vices.

On the contrary, Augustine says in his work *On Free Choice*: "It seems to me that laws written for the people's governance rightly permit such things, and that God's providence punishes them."[17] But God's providence only punishes sins. Therefore, human laws, by not prohibiting some sins, rightly permit them.

I answer that laws are established as the rules or measures of human actions, as I have already said.[18] But measures should be homogeneous with what they measure, as the *Metaphysics* says,[19] since different kinds of things are measured by different kinds of measures. And so laws need also to be imposed on human beings according to their condition, since laws ought to be "possible regarding both nature and a country's customs," as Isidore says.[20] And the power or ability to act results from internal habituation or disposition, since the virtuous and those without virtuous habits do not have the same power to act. Just so, children and adults do not have the same power to act, and so the law is not the same for children and adults. For example, many things are permitted children that the law punishes in adults, or even that public opinion censures. And likewise, many things are tolerated in persons of imperfect virtue that would not be tolerated in virtuous persons.

And human law is established for the collectivity of human beings, most of whom have imperfect virtue. And so human law does not prohibit every kind of vice, from which the virtuous abstain. Rather, human law prohibits only the more serious kinds of vice, from which most persons can abstain, and especially those vices that inflict harm on others, without the prohibition of which human society could not be preserved. For example, human laws prohibit murders, thefts, and the like.

Reply Obj. 1. Audacity seems to belong to attacks on others. And so audacity belongs chiefly to the sins that inflict injury on neighbors, and human law prohibits such sins, as I have said.[21]

---

[16]I–II, Q. 95, A. 2.   [17]*On Free Choice* I, 5, n. 13 (PL 32:1228).   [18]I–II, Q. 90, AA. 1, 2.   [19]*Metaphysics* X, 1 (1053a24–30).   [20]*Etymologies* II, 10 (PL 82:131); V, 21 (PL 82:203).   [21]In the body of the article.

Reply Obj. 2. Human laws aim to induce human beings to virtue little by little, not all at once. And so the laws do not immediately impose on the many imperfect citizens what already belongs to virtuous citizens, namely, that citizens abstain from everything evil. Otherwise, the imperfect citizens, unable to endure those commands, would erupt into worse evil things. Just so, Prov. 30:33 says: "Those who blow their nose too strongly, emit blood." And Mt. 9:17 says: "If one should put new wine," that is, the precepts of a perfect life, "into old wineskins," that is, imperfect human beings, "the wineskins burst, and the wine is spilled," that is, the precepts are despised, and human beings burst into worse evil things out of contempt.

Reply Obj. 3. The natural law is our participation in the eternal law, but human law falls short of the eternal law. For Augustine says in his work *On Free Choice:* "The laws framed for the governance of political communities permit and leave unpunished many things that God's providence punishes. Nor, indeed, should we criticize what the laws do do because of the fact that they do not do everything." [22] And so also human laws cannot prohibit everything that the natural law prohibits.

THIRD ARTICLE
Do Human Laws Command Every Virtuous Action?

We thus proceed to the third inquiry. It seems that human laws do not command every virtuous action, for the following reasons:

Objection 1. Vicious actions are the contrary of virtuous actions. But human laws do not prohibit all vices, as I have said. [23] Therefore, human laws also do not command every virtuous action.

Obj. 2. Virtuous actions come from virtue. But virtue is the aim of laws, and so what comes from virtue cannot fall within legal precepts. Therefore, human laws do not command every virtuous action.

Obj. 3. Laws are ordained for the common good, as I have said. [24] But some virtuous actions are ordained for private, not the common, good. Therefore, laws do not command every virtuous action.

On the contrary, the Philosopher says in the *Ethics:* "Laws command courageous and temperate and gentle behavior, and likewise regarding other virtues and vices, commanding the former and fobidding the latter." [25]

I answer that we distinguish specific virtues by their objects, as is evident from what I have said before. [26] But we can relate all the objects of

---

[22] *On Free Choice* I, 5, n. 13 (PL 32:1228).   [23] A. 2.   [24] I–II, Q. 90, A. 2.
[25] *Ethics* V, 1 (1129b19–25).   [26] I–II: Q. 54, A. 2; Q. 60, A. 1; Q. 62, A. 2.

virtues either to the private good of a person or to the common good of the people. For example, one can perform courageous acts either to preserve the political community or to uphold the rights of one's friends, and similarly with other virtuous acts. And laws are ordained for the common good, as I have said.[27] And so there are no virtues regarding whose actions laws could not command. But laws do not command regarding every action of every virtue. Rather, they only command things that can be ordained for the common good, whether immediately, as when things are done directly for that good, or mediately, as when lawmakers ordain things belonging to good training, which trains citizens to preserve the common good of justice and peace.

Reply Obj. 1. Human laws do not by strict command prohibit every vicious action, just as they do not command every virtuous action. But human laws prohibit some acts of particular vices, just as they command some acts of particular virtues.

Reply Obj. 2. We call actions virtuous in two ways. We call them virtuous in one way because persons perform virtuous deeds. For example, just actions consist of doing just things, brave actions consist of doing brave things. And human laws command virtuous acts in this way. We call actions virtuous in a second way because persons perform virtuous deeds as virtuous persons do. And the actions of virtuous persons always come from virtue and do not fall within legal precepts, although lawmakers aim to induce such behavior.

Reply Obj. 3. There are no virtues whose actions cannot be ordained for the common good, either directly or indirectly, as I have said.[28]

FOURTH ARTICLE
Does Human Law Impose Obligation on Human Beings in the Court of Conscience?

We thus proceed to the fourth inquiry. It seems that human law does not impose obligation on human beings in the court of conscience, for the following reasons:

Objection 1. Lower powers cannot impose laws on the courts of higher powers. But the power of human beings, which establishes human laws, is inferior to God's power. Therefore, human law cannot impose laws on the court of God, that is, the court of conscience.

Obj. 2. The judgment of conscience depends most of all on God's commandments. But human laws sometimes nullify God's commandments, as Mt. 15:6 says: "You have nullified God's commandment for the sake of

---

[27]I–II, Q. 90, A. 2.   [28]In the body of the article.

your traditions." Therefore, human laws do not impose obligation regarding conscience.

Obj. 3. Human laws often bring defamation and injury to human beings. Just so, Is. 10:1-2 says: "Woe to those who establish wicked laws and inscribe injustices when they write laws, in order to oppress the poor in the courts and do violence in cases involving the lowly of my people." But all are permitted to avoid oppression and violence. Therefore, human laws do not impose obligation on human beings regarding conscience.

On the contrary, 1 Pet. 2:19 says: "It is a blessing if one, suffering unjustly, endures sorrows for the sake of conscience."

I answer that laws established by human beings are either just or unjust. If just, they indeed have obligatory force in the court of conscience from the eternal law, from which they are derived. Just so, Prov. 8:15 says: "Kings rule through me, and lawmakers decree justice." And we call laws just from three perspectives: (1) from their end, namely, when they are ordained for the common good; (2) from their authority, namely, when the laws enacted do not surpass the power of the lawmakers; (3) from their form, namely, when they impose proportionately equal burdens on citizens for the common good.

And laws are unjust in two ways. They are unjust in one way by being contrary to the human good in the foregoing respects. Laws may be unjust regarding their end, as when authorities impose burdensome laws on citizens to satisfy the authorities' covetousness or vainglory rather than to benefit the community. Or laws may be unjust regarding the authority to make them, as when persons enact laws that exceed the power committed to them. Or laws may be unjust regarding their form, as when burdens, even if ordained for the common good, are disproportionately imposed on the people. And such laws are acts of violence rather than laws, since "unjust laws do not seem to be laws," as Augustine says in his work *On Free Choice*.[29] And so such laws do not oblige in the court of conscience, except perhaps to avoid scandal or civil unrest, to avoid which human beings ought to yield even their rights. Just so, Mt. 5:40-41 says: "If someone has taken your coat from you, give the person your cloak as well, and if someone has forced you to go one mile, go with the person another two."

Laws can be unjust in a second way by being contrary to the divine good (e.g., the laws of tyrants inducing their subjects to worship idols or to do anything else contrary to the divine law). And it is never permissible to obey such laws, since "we ought to obey God rather than human beings," as Acts 5:29 says.

---

[29] *On Free Choice* I, 5, n. 11 (PL 32:1227).

Reply Obj. 1. The Apostle says in Rom. 13:1–2: "All human power is from God, and so those who resist the power" in matters belonging to its scope "resist God's ordination." And so such persons become guilty in respect to their conscience.

Reply Obj. 2. The argument of this objection is valid about human laws ordained contrary to God's commandments. And the scope of human power does not extend to such laws. And so one should not obey human laws in such matters.

Reply Obj. 3. The argument of this objection is valid about laws that inflict unjust burdens on citizens, and also the scope of power granted by God does not extend to such laws. And so human beings are not obliged in such cases to obey the laws if it be possible to resist them without giving scandal or causing greater harm.

FIFTH ARTICLE
Is Everyone Subject to the Law?

We thus proceed to the fifth inquiry. It seems that not everyone is subject to the law, for the following reasons:

Objection 1. Only those for whom laws are established are subject to the law. But the Apostle says in 1 Tim. 1:9 that "laws are not established for the righteous." Therefore, the righteous are not subject to human law.

Obj. 2. Pope Urban says, and the *Decretum* maintains: "No reason demands that those guided by private law be constrained by public law." [30] But all spiritual persons, who are sons and daughters of God, are guided by the private law of the Holy Spirit. Just so, Rom. 8:14 says: "Those moved by the Spirit of God are God's children." Therefore, not every person is subject to human law.

Obj. 3. The Jurist says that "rulers are exempt from the laws." [31] But those exempt from the law are not subject to it. Therefore, not everyone is subject to the law.

On the contrary, the Apostle says in Rom. 13:1: "Let every soul be subject to higher powers." But any persons not subject to the law that higher powers establish seem not to be subject to the powers. Therefore, all persons should be subject to human law.

I answer that, as is evident from what I have said before, [32] two things belong to the nature of law: first, indeed, that law be the rule of human actions; second, that law have coercive power. Therefore, human beings can be subject to the law in two ways. They can be subject to law in one

---

[30] Gratian, *Decretum* II, cause 19, q. 2, c. 2. [31] *Digest* I, title 3, law 31.
[32] I–II, Q. 90, AA. 1, 2; A. 3, *ad* 2.

way as the ones regulated by the rule. And in this regard, all those subject to a power are subject to the laws the power establishes. But one may not be subject to a power in two ways. One may not be subject to a power in one way because one is absolutely free from subjection to the power. And so those belonging to one political community or kingdom are not subject to the laws of the ruler of another political community or kingdom, since such persons are not subject to that ruler's dominion. One may not be subject to a power in a second way insofar as one is ruled by a higher law. For example, a person subject to a proconsul ought to be ruled by the proconsul's commands but not regarding matters from which the emperor exempted the person. For regarding the latter, a person directed by a higher command is not bound by the command of an inferior power. And so those absolutely subject to the law may not be bound by the law regarding matters about which they are ruled by a higher law.

We say in a second way that some are subject to the law as the coerced to the power coercing. And in this respect, only the wicked, not the virtuous and righteous, are subject to the law. For what is coerced and forced is contrary to the will. But the will of the virtuous is in accord, and the will of the wicked in discord, with the law. And so only the wicked, not the virtuous, are subject to the law in this respect.

Reply Obj. 1. The argument of this objection is valid about being subject to the law by way of coercion. For then "the law is not established for the righteous," since "they are a law unto themselves" because "they manifest what the law requires written in their hearts," as the Apostle says in Rom. 2:14–15. And so the law does not have the coercive force in their regard that the law has regarding the wicked.

Reply Obj. 2. The law of the Holy Spirit is superior to every human law. And so spiritual persons, insofar as they are guided by the law of the Holy Spirit, are not subject to human law regarding things contrary to the Holy Spirit's guidance. But it belongs to the Holy Spirit's guidance that spiritual persons be subject to human laws, as 1 Pet. 2:13 says: "Be subject to every human creature for God's sake."

Reply Obj. 3. We say that rulers are exempt from the law regarding its coercive force, since, properly speaking, one is not coerced by oneself, and law has coercive force only by the power of a ruler. Therefore, we say that rulers are exempt from the law because no one can pass sentence on them if they act contrary to the law. And so a gloss on Ps. 51:4, "I have sinned against you alone," etc., says that "there is no one who is competent to judge the deeds of a king."[33]

---

[33]*Glossa ordinaria*, on Ps. 51:4 (PL 113:919); Peter Lombard, *Glossa*, on Ps. 51:4 (PL 191:486).

But regarding the directive power of law, rulers are subject to the law by their own will. Just so, the *Decretals* say: "Rulers should follow the law that they decree for others. And the authority of a wise man says: 'Obey the law you yourself decreed.'[34]"[35] Also, the Lord reproves "those who preach and do not practice" and "those who impose heavy burdens on others but do not themselves want to lift a finger to move them," as Mt. 23:3–4 relates. And so, regarding God's judgment, rulers are not exempt from the law regarding its directive power, and they should willingly, not by coercion, fulfill the law.

Also, rulers are above the law insofar as they can, if it be expedient, alter the law and dispense from it at certain times and places.

SIXTH ARTICLE
Are Those Subject to the Law Permitted to Act Contrary to the Letter of the Law?

We thus proceed to the sixth inquiry. It seems that those subject to the law are not permitted to act contrary to the letter of the law, for the following reasons:

Objection 1. Augustine says in his work *On True Religion:* "Although human beings judge about temporal laws when they decree them, the subjects will not be permitted to judge about them after they have been decreed and established. Rather, subjects should judge according to the laws."[36] But if one disregards the letter of the law, claiming that one preserves the lawmaker's aim, such a one seems to judge about the law. Therefore, those subject to the law are not permitted to disregard the letter of the law in order to preserve the lawmaker's aim.

Obj. 2. Only those who frame laws are competent to interpret them. But human beings subject to the law are not competent to frame them. Therefore, such human beings are not competent to interpret them. Rather, such human beings ought always to act according to the letter of the law.

Obj. 3. Every wise person knows how to explain the person's aim in words. But we ought to esteem wise those who frame laws, since wisdom says in Prov. 8:15: "Kings rule through me, and the framers of laws decree justice." Therefore, we should judge about the lawmaker's aim only by the words of the law.

---

[34]Denis Cato, *Concise Opinions and Distichs on Morals*, preliminary opinion 53.
[35]Gregory IX, *Decretals* I, title 2, c. 6.   [36]*On True Religion* 31 (PL 34:148).

On the contrary, Hilary says in his work *On the Trinity:* "We should understand the meaning of statements from the reasons for making them, since speech ought to be governed by things, not things by speech."[37] Therefore, we ought to pay more attention to the lawmaker's aim than to the very words of the law.

I answer that, as I have said before,[38] every law is ordained for the commonweal and has the force and nature of law insofar as it is so ordained. But a law has no power to bind morally insofar as it falls short of this ordination. And so the Jurist says: "No aspect of law or favor of equity allows us to render severe by a harsher interpretation contrary to the benefit of human beings things wholesomely introduced for their benefit."[39] And it often happens that observing the law is generally beneficial to the commonweal but most harmful to it in particular cases. Therefore, since lawmakers cannot envision all particular cases, they direct their aim at the common benefit and establish laws regarding things that generally happen. And so one should not observe a law if a case happens to arise in which observance of the law would be harmful to the commonweal. For example, if a law should decree that the gates of a besieged city remain shut, this is for the most part for the benefit of the commonweal. But if a situation should arise in which enemy soldiers are pursuing some citizens defending the city, it would be most harmful to the community if the gates were not to be opened to admit the defenders. And so, contrary to the letter of the law, the city gates should be opened in such a situation in order to preserve the commonweal, which is the lawmaker's intention.

And yet we should note that not everyone is competent to interpret what may be useful or not useful for the community if observance of the letter of the law does not risk a sudden danger that needs to be immediately resolved. Rather, only rulers are competent to make such interpretations, and they have authority in such cases to dispense citizens from laws. On the other hand, if there be a sudden danger that does not allow enough time to be able to have recourse to a superior, the very necessity includes an implicit dispensation, since necessity is not subject to the law.

Reply Obj. 1. Those who in cases of necessity act contrary to the letter of the law do not judge about the law itself. Rather, they judge about particular cases, in which they perceive that they should not observe the letter of the law.

Reply Obj. 2. Those who follow the lawmaker's aim do not, absolutely speaking, interpret the law. Rather, they interpret the law regarding

---

[37] *On the Trinity* IV, n. 14 (PL 10:107).   [38] A. 4.   [39] *Digest* I, title 3, law 25.

particular cases in which evidence of harm makes it clear that the law-maker intended otherwise than the letter of the law. For if they have any doubt, they ought to act according to the letter of the law or consult superiors.

Reply Obj. 3. No human being's wisdom is so great as to be able to contemplate every single case. And so one cannot adequately express in words the things suitable for an intended end. And if a lawmaker could contemplate all cases, the lawmaker, to avoid confusing citizens, need not express all of them. Rather, the lawmaker should establish laws regarding what generally happens.

QUESTION 97
On Revision of Laws

FIRST ARTICLE
Should Human Law Be Revised in Any Way?

We thus proceed to the first inquiry. It seems that human law should be revised in no way, for the following reasons:

Objection 1. Human law is derived from the natural law, as I have said before.[1] But the natural law remains immutable. Therefore, human law ought to remain immutable.

Obj. 2. Measures ought to be most permanent, as the Philosopher says in the *Ethics*.[2] But human law is the measure of human actions, as I have said before.[3] Therefore, human law ought to remain without change.

Obj. 3. It belongs to the nature of law to be just and upright, as I have said before.[4] But things once upright are always upright. Therefore, things once law ought always to be law.

On the contrary, Augustine says in his work *On Free Choice:* "Temporal law, although just, can be justly revised over time."[5]

I answer that, as I have said before,[6] human law is a dictate of reason directing human actions. And so there can be two reasons why laws may be rightly revised: one, indeed, regarding reason; the second regarding human beings, whose actions laws regulate. One reason indeed regards reason, since it seems to be natural for reason to advance step-by-step from the imperfect to the perfect. And so we perceive, regarding theoretical sciences, that the first philosophers transmitted imperfect doctrines that later philosophers corrected. So also is this the case in practical matters. For the first lawmakers, who strove to discover things useful for the human community but were unable of themselves to contemplate everything, instituted imperfect laws that were deficient in many respects. And later lawmakers revised those laws, establishing laws that could fail to serve the commonweal in fewer cases.

And regarding human beings, whose actions laws regulate, laws can be rightly revised to suit the changed conditions of human beings, and different things are expedient for human beings according to their different

---

[1] I–II, Q. 95, A. 2.   [2] *Ethics* V, 5 (1133a25).   [3] I–II, Q. 90, AA. 1, 2.
[4] I–II, Q. 90, A. 2.   [5] *On Free Choice* I, 6, n. 14 (PL 32:1229).   [6] I–II, Q. 91, A. 3.

circumstances. Just so, Augustine in his work *On Free Choice* poses this example:

> If a people should be well-tempered and serious and most diligently mindful of the commonweal, a law is rightly framed that permits such a people to choose magistrates to administer the commonwealth. Then, if the same people, corrupted over time, sell their votes and entrust their governance to scoundrels and criminals, the power to bestow offices is rightly taken away from such a people, and the power to bestow the offices falls to the choice of a few good persons.[7]

Reply Obj. 1. The natural law is a participation in the eternal law, as I have said before,[8] and so the natural law remains immutable. And the natural law has this immutability from the immutability and perfection of the divine reason that establishes human nature. But human reason is mutable and imperfect.

And besides, the natural law consists of universal precepts that always abide, while laws established by human beings consist of particular precepts that regard different situations that arise.

Reply Obj. 2. Measures ought to be as permanent as possible. But there cannot be anything altogether immutably permanent in mutable things. And so human laws cannot be altogether immutable.

Reply Obj. 3. We predicate upright of material things in an absolute sense, and so they stay upright as far as it is in their power. But we speak of the rectitude of laws in relation to the commonweal, to which the same things are not always duly proportionate, as I have said before.[9] And so such rectitude changes.

SECOND ARTICLE
Should Human Laws Always Be Revised for Something Better?

We thus proceed to the second inquiry. It seems that human laws should always be revised for something better, for the following reasons:

Objection 1. Human reason devises human laws, just as it devises human skills. But prior rules regarding other skills are modified for better rules. Therefore, we should also do the same regarding human laws.

Obj. 2. We can provide for the future from things of the past. But many unsuitable things would result if human laws were not revised by adding better provisions, since the laws of antiquity were unsophisticated in many respects. Therefore, it seems that laws should be revised as often as something better presents itself to be made law.

---

[7] *On Free Choice* I, 6, n. 14 (PL 32:1229).   [8] I–II: Q. 91, A. 2; Q. 96, A. 2, *ad* 3.
[9] In the body of the article.

Obj. 3. Human laws are framed for the particular actions of human beings. But regarding such actions, we can gain complete knowledge only by experience, which "takes time," as the *Ethics* says.[10] Therefore, it seems that better things can occur over time and should be enacted as laws.

On the contrary, the *Decretum* says: "It is foolish and rather detestably shameful to allow the tradtions of our forefathers to be modified."[11]

I answer that, as I have said,[12] human laws are revised insofar as their revision serves the commonweal. But the very revision of laws, considered as such, involves some detriment to the commonweal. For custom avails very much for the observance of laws, since we regard things done contrary to common custom, even if those things be in themselves slight, as rather serious. And so the binding force of law is diminished when laws are revised, since custom is removed. And so human laws should never be revised unless the commonweal gains in one respect as much as it loses in the other. And such indeed is the case either because a very great and very clear benefit results from the new law, or because there is a very great necessity due either to the fact that the existing law is clearly unjust, or to the fact that observance of the existing law is most harmful. And so the Jurist says that "in establishing new laws, the benefit of departing from laws long perceived as just ought to be evident."[13]

Reply Obj. 1. The rules relating to skills derive their efficacy only from reason, and so prior rules should be revised whenever a better reason presents itself. But "laws have their greatest power from custom," as the Philosopher says in the *Politics*.[14] And so we should not rush to revise laws.

Reply Obj. 2. The argument of this objection rightly concludes that laws should be revised. But they should be revised for the sake of a great benefit or necessity, not for the sake of any betterment, as I have said.[15]

Reply Obj. 3. The same argument applies to this objection.

THIRD ARTICLE
Can Customs Obtain the Force of Law?

We thus proceed to the third inquiry. It seems that customs cannot obtain the force of law or abolish laws, for the following reasons:

Objection 1. Human law is derived from the natural law and the divine law, as is evident from what I have said before.[16] But human customs cannot alter the natural law or the divine law. Therefore, they also cannot alter human law.

---

[10]*Ethics* II, 1 (1103a16).   [11]Gratian, *Decretum* I, dist. 12, c. 5.   [12]A. 1.
[13]*Digest* I, title 4, law 2.   [14]*Politics* II, 5 (1269a20–24).   [15]In the body of the article.   [16]I–II: Q. 93, A. 3; Q. 95, A. 2.

Obj. 2. Moral good cannot come out of many wicked acts. But those who first begin to act contrary to a law act wickedly. Therefore, many such acts do not produce something morally good. But law is something morally good, since law regulates human actions. Therefore, customs cannot abolish laws so that the customs obtain the force of law.

Obj. 3. Framing laws belongs to public persons, whose business it is to govern a community, and so private persons cannot make law. But customs flourish through the acts of private persons. Therefore, custom cannot obtain the force of law so as to abolish laws.

On the contrary, Augustine says in a letter: "We should consider the customs of God's people and the prescriptions of our ancestors as laws. And as those who disobey God's laws should be punished, so also should those who contemn the Church's customs."[17]

I answer that all laws come from the reason and will of lawmakers: the divine and natural laws, indeed, from the reasonable will of God, and human laws from human wills regulated by reason. But the deeds of human beings as much as their words indicate their reason and will regarding things to be done. For example, everyone seems to desire as good what one carries out in deed. And human words evidently alter and also explain laws insofar as the words explain the internal movements and thoughts of human reason. And so also even acts, especially when repeated so as to constitute custom, can alter and explain laws, and cause things to obtain the force of law, namely, insofar as repeated external acts most effectively manifest internal movements of the will and the thoughts of reason. For things done repeatedly seem to proceed from deliberate judgments of reason. And so custom both has the force of law and abolishes law and interprets law.

Reply Obj. 1. The natural law and the divine law come from the divine will, as I have said.[18] And so only divine authority, not customs that come from the will of human beings, can alter those laws. And so no custom can obtain the force of law in opposition to the divine and natural laws, as Isidore says in his *Synonyms*: "Let custom yield to authority; let law and reason prevail over wicked customs."[19]

Reply Obj. 2. Human laws are wanting in particular cases, as I have said before.[20] And so one can sometimes act outside the law, namely, in cases in which the laws are wanting, and yet the actions will not be morally evil. And when such instances are repeated because of alterations in human beings, then customs indicate that laws are no longer useful, just

---

[17]*Letter 36*, to Casulanus (PL 33:136). [18]In the body of the article.
[19]*Synonyms* II, n. 80 (PL 83:863).   [20]I–II, Q. 96, A. 6.

as it would be evident that laws are no longer useful if expressly contrary laws were to be promulgated. But if the same reason for which the original law was useful still persists, the law prevails over the custom, not the custom over the law. There may be an exception if the law seems useless simply because it is not "possible according to a country's customs," which was one of the conditions of law.[21] For it is difficult to destroy a people's customs.

Reply Obj. 3. The people among whom a custom is introduced can be in two situations. For if a people is free, that is, self-governing, the consent of the whole people, which custom indicates, counts more in favor of a particular legal observance than the authority of its ruler, who only has the power to frame laws insofar as the ruler acts in the name of the people. And so the whole people can establish laws, but individual persons cannot.

But if a people should not have the free disposition to frame laws for itself or to abolish laws imposed by a higher power, the very customs prevailing in such a people still obtain the force of law insofar as those who have the power to impose laws on the people tolerate the customs. For rulers thereby seem to approve what the customs introduce.

FOURTH ARTICLE
Can the People's Rulers Dispense Subjects from Human Laws?

We thus proceed to the fourth inquiry. It seems that the people's rulers cannot dispense subjects from human laws, for the following reasons:

Objection 1. Laws are established "for the commonweal," as Isidore says.[22] But the common good should not be cast aside for the private convenience of a particular person, since "the good of the people is more godlike than the good of one human being," as the Philosopher says in the *Ethics*.[23] Therefore, it seems that no one should be dispensed to act contrary to the people's common law.

Obj. 2. Dt. 1:17 commands those with authority over others: "You shall listen to the lowly as well as the mighty, nor shall you regard who anyone is, since your judgment is God's." But to grant to one what is denied to all seems to be regard for who the person is. Therefore, the people's rulers cannot give such dispensations, since this is contrary to a precept of the divine law.

Obj. 3. Human law, if just, needs to be in accord with the natural and divine laws; otherwise, it would not "be fitting for religion" or "be suitable for training," which are prerequisites of law, as Isidore says.[24] But

---

[21] I–II, Q. 95, A. 3.   [22] *Etymologies* II, 10 (PL 82:131); V, 3 (PL 82:199).
[23] *Ethics* I, 2 (1094b9–10).   [24] *Etymologies* II, 10 (PL 82:131); V, 3 (PL 82:199).

no human being can dispense anyone from the divine and natural laws. Therefore, neither can any human being dispense someone from a human law.

On the contrary, the Apostle says in 1 Cor. 9:17: "Dispensation has been entrusted to me."

I answer that dispensing, properly speaking, signifies allotting common goods to individuals. And so we also call the heads of households dispensers, since they with due weight and in due measure distribute to each member of their households both duties and things necessary for living. Therefore, we also say regarding any political community that one dispenses, since that one in a way ordains how individuals should fulfill a general precept. And a precept generally for the convenience of the community may sometimes be unsuitable for a particular person or in a particular case, either because it would prevent something better, or because it would even bring about some evil, as is evident from what I have said before.[25] But it would be most dangerous to commit this to the discretion of each individual, except, perhaps, when there is a clear and present danger, as I have said before.[26] And so those empowered to rule a people have the power to dispense from human laws that rest on the rulers' authority, namely, as regards persons or situations in which the law is wanting, to grant permission not to observe precepts of the law.

But if rulers should grant this permission at their mere whim, without the persons or situations warranting it, they will be unfaithful or unwise dispensers. Rulers will be unfaithful dispensers if they do not aim at the common good, and they will be unwise dispensers if they ignore the reason for granting dispensations. And so the Lord says in Lk. 12:42: "Who, do you think, is the faithful and wise dispenser that a master sets over his household?"

Reply Obj. 1. One ought not to be dispensed from observing general laws at the prejudice of the common good. Rather, dispensations should be granted for the purpose of benefiting the common good.

Reply Obj. 2. There is no regard for who persons are if unequal things are dispensed to persons who are unequal. And so when the condition of persons requires that special things be reasonably accorded them, there is no regard for who the persons are if special favors are granted them.

Reply Obj. 3. The natural law as consisting of general precepts, which are never wanting, cannot be dispensed. But human beings sometimes dispense from other precepts of the natural law, which are quasi-conclusions

---

[25]I–II, Q. 96, A. 6.   [26]Ibid.

from the general precepts (e.g., dispensing from the obligation to repay loans owed to traitors, or the like).

But every human being is subject to the divine law as private persons are subject to public law. And so, as only rulers or their representatives can dispense from human laws, so only God or his special representatives can dispense from precepts of the divine law.

[Questions 98–105 deal with the Old Law. Questions 106–108 deal with the New Law and its relation to the Old Law. Only AA. 1–3, 8–12 of Q. 100 and A. 1 of Q. 105 are translated here.]

QUESTION 100

On the Moral Precepts of the Old Law

FIRST ARTICLE
Do All the Moral Precepts of the Old
Law Belong to the Natural Law?

We thus proceed to the first inquiry. It seems that not every moral precept of the Old Law belongs to the natural law, for the following reasons:

Objection 1. Sir. 17:9 says: "In addition, he [God] bequeathed them instruction and the law that brings life." But we contradistinguish instruction from the natural law, since we do not learn that law. Rather, we know that law by an impulse from nature. Therefore, not every moral precept of the Old Law belongs to the natural law.

Obj. 2. The divine law is more complete than human law. But human law adds things pertaining to good morals to things belonging to the natural law. And this is evidenced by the fact that the natural law is the same for all human beings, but the things pertaining to good morals established by human law are different for different peoples. Therefore, there was a much stronger reason why the divine law should have added to the natural law things pertaining to good morals.

Obj. 3. As natural reason leads human beings to particular good morals, so also does faith. And so also Gal. 5:6 says that "faith acts through charity." But faith is not contained in the natural law, since things belonging to faith surpass natural reason. Therefore, not every moral precept of the divine law belongs to the natural law.

On the contrary, the Apostle says in Rom. 2:14: "The Gentiles, who do not have the [Old] Law, by nature do the things belonging to the Law." But we need to understand this about things pertaining to good morals. Therefore, all the moral precepts of the Old Law belong to the natural law.

I answer that moral precepts of the Old Law, as distinguished from its ceremonial precepts and its precepts governing the administration of jus-

70

tice, concern things that as such belong to good morals. And since we speak of human morals in relation to reason, which is the specific source of human acts, we call those morals good that are in accord with reason, and those morals bad that are not. And as every judgment of theoretical reason derives from the natural knowledge of first principles, so also every judgment of practical reason derives from certain naturally known first principles, as I have said before.[1] And one can in various ways proceed from these principles to judge about different things.

For example, there are some things regarding human acts so explicit that, by applying the general and first principles, we can with rather little reflection at once approve or disapprove them. And there are some things that, in order to be judged morally, require much reflection on various circumstances, which only the wise, not everyone, is qualified to study carefully. Just so, considering particular scientific conclusions belongs only to philosophers, not to everybody. And there are some things that human beings need the help of divine instruction in order to judge, as is the case regarding articles of faith.

But the moral precepts of the Old Law concern things that pertain to good morals, and such precepts are in accord with reason. And every judgment of human reason is derived from natural reason. Therefore, all the moral precepts of the Old Law evidently need to belong to the natural law, albeit in different ways.

For example, the natural reason of each person at once judges that some things as such are to be done or not to be done (e.g., "Honor thy father and thy mother,"[2] "Thou shalt not kill,"[3] "Thou shalt not steal"[4]). And such precepts belong to the natural law absolutely.

And there are some things that the wise after more careful reflection judge should be done. And these things belong to the natural law but in such a way that they need instruction, whereby the wiser teach those less wise (e.g., "Rise up at the presence of a grey head, and honor the person of the elderly,"[5] and such like).

And there are some things that human reason needs divine instruction to judge, and we thereby learn about divine things (e.g., "Thou shalt not make for thyself a graven image or any likeness,"[6] "Thou shalt not take the name of the Lord thy God in vain"[7]).

Reply Objs. 1–3. And this answer makes clear the replies to the objections.

---

[1] I–II, Q. 94, AA. 2, 4.   [2] Ex. 20:12; Dt. 5:16.   [3] Ex. 20:13; Dt. 5:17.
[4] Ex. 20:15; Dt. 5:19.   [5] Lev. 19:32   [6] Ex. 20:4; Dt. 5:8.   [7] Ex. 20:7;
Dt. 5:11.

SECOND ARTICLE
Do the Moral Precepts of the Old
Law Concern All Virtuous Acts?

We thus proceed to the second inquiry. It seems that the moral precepts of the Old Law do not concern all virtuous acts, for the following reasons:

Objection 1. We call observance of the precepts of the Old Law justification, as Ps. 119:8 says: "I shall observe your ways of justification." But justification is the execution of justice. Therefore, the moral precepts of the Old Law concern only acts of justice.

Obj. 2. What falls under a precept has the nature of something owed. But the nature of something owed belongs only to justice, whose particular act is to render to everyone what is owed to that person, and not to other virtues. Therefore, the moral precepts of the Old Law concern only acts of justice, not the acts of other virtues.

Obj. 3. Every law is established for the common good, as Isidore says.[8] But of virtues, only justice regards the common good, as the Philosopher says in the *Ethics*.[9] Therefore, the moral precepts of the Old Law concern only justice.

On the contrary, Ambrose says that "sin is transgression of the divine law and disobedience of the heavenly commandments."[10] But sins run contrary to all virtuous acts. Therefore, the divine law has ordinances regarding all virtuous acts.

I answer that since legal precepts are ordained for the common good, as I have maintained before,[11] they need to be distinguished by different kinds of political communities. And so also the Philosopher teaches in the *Politics* that one kind of laws needs to be framed for a political community ruled by a king, and a different kind of laws needs to be framed for a political community where the people or some powerful persons in the community rule.[12] And there is one kind of community for which human law is ordained, and another kind for which divine law is ordained.

For human law is ordained for a political community, which consists of human beings in relation to one another. And human beings are related to one another by external actions, whereby they are in communion with one another. And such communion belongs to the nature of justice, which, properly speaking, gives direction to a human community. And so human law lays down precepts only regarding acts of justice, and it pre-

---

[8] *Etymologies* II, 10 (PL 82:131); V, 21 (PL 82:203). [9] *Ethics* V, 1 (1130a3–5).
[10] *On Paradise* 8 (PL 14:292).   [11] I–II, Q. 90, A. 2.   [12] *Politics* IV, 1 (1289a11–25).

scribes other virtuous acts, if at all, only insofar as those acts take on an aspect of justice, as the Philosopher makes clear in the *Ethics*.[13]

But the community for which divine law provides consists of human beings in relation to God, whether in the present or the future life. And so divine law lays down precepts regarding everything that rightly orders human beings for communion with God. But human beings are united to God by their reason or mind, in which is the image of God. And so the divine law lays down precepts about everything that rightly orders human beings' reason. And all virtuous acts bring this about. For example, intellectual virtues rightly order acts of reason, as such, and moral virtues rightly order acts of reason regarding internal emotions and external actions. And so the divine law fittingly lays down precepts about the acts of every virtue. But the divine law does so in such a way that some things, without which the order of virtue, that is, the order of reason, cannot be observed, fall under the obligation of precepts, while things belonging to the well-being of complete virtue fall under the admonition of counsels.

Reply Obj. 1. Keeping the commandments of the Old Law even regarding the acts of virtues other than justice has the nature of justification, since it is just that human beings obey God, or even that everything belonging to human beings be subject to reason.

Reply Obj. 2. Justice, properly speaking, concerns what one human being owes to another, but every other virtue concerns the duty lower powers owe to reason. And by reason of such duty, the Philosopher in the *Ethics* speaks of justice in a metaphorical sense.[14]

Reply Obj. 3. What I have said about different kinds of community makes clear the reply to this objection.[15]

THIRD ARTICLE
Do We Trace All the Moral Precepts of the Old Law to the Ten Commandments?

We thus proceed to the third inquiry. It seems that we do not trace all the moral precepts of the Old Law to the Ten Commandments, for the following reasons:

Objection 1. As Mt. 22:37, 39 says, the first and chief precepts of the Old Law are: "Thou shalt love the Lord thy God" and "Thou shalt love thy neighbor." But these two precepts are not included in the Decalogue.

---

[13] *Ethics* V, 1 (1129b12–25).   [14] Ibid. V, 11 (1138b5–14).   [15] In the body of the article.

Therefore, not all the moral precepts of the Old Law are included in the Decalogue.

Obj. 2. We do not trace the moral precepts of the Old Law to its ceremonial precepts. Rather, we do the converse. But one of the commandments, namely, "Remember that thou keep holy the Sabbath,"[16] is ceremonial. Therefore, we do not trace all the moral precepts of the Old Law to all the commandments of the Decalogue.

Obj. 3. The moral precepts of the Old Law concern all virtuous acts. But the Decalogue includes only precepts pertaining to acts of justice, as is evident to anyone who examines them one by one. Therefore, the Decalogue does not include all the moral precepts of the Old Law.

On the contrary, a gloss on Mt. 5:11, "Blessed are you when they have reviled you," etc., says that Moses, after laying down the Ten Commandments, explains them in particulars.[17] Therefore, all the precepts of the Old Law are particulars of the Decalogue.

I answer that the Decalogue differs from the other precepts of the Old Law in that God himself is said to have laid down the Decalogue for the people but laid down the other precepts for them through Moses. And the precepts whose knowledge human beings possess from God himself belong to the Decalogue. But the precepts they can know from the first general principles with rather little reflection, as well as those divinely infused faith reveals, are such. Therefore, two kinds of precepts are not reckoned among the precepts of the Decalogue. The first kind consists of the first and general precepts, and these precepts need no further promulgation than their inscription on natural reason as self-evident, as it were (e.g., human beings should do evil to no one, and such like). And the second kind consists of the precepts that the wise by careful study discover belong to reason, since God communicates these precepts to the people through the instruction of the wise. Still, both of these kinds of precepts are included in the Decalogue, albeit in different ways. For the first and general precepts are included as first principles in proximate conclusions, and, conversely, the precepts known through the wise are included as conclusions in first principles.

Reply Obj. 1. These two precepts are first and general precepts of the natural law self-evident to human reason, whether by nature or by faith. And so all precepts of the Decalogue are traceable to these two precepts as conclusions to general first principles.

Reply Obj. 2. The commandment to observe the Sabbath is moral in one respect, namely, that human beings devote some time to divine things,

---

[16]Ex. 20:8; Dt. 5:12.   [17]*Glossa ordinaria*, on Mt. 5:11 (PL 114:90).

as Ps. 46:10 says: "Be still and perceive that I am God." And we reckon the commandment to observe the Sabbath among the moral precepts of the Decalogue in this respect, but not as to the appointed day, since the commandment in the latter respect is ceremonial.

Reply Obj. 3. The nature of obligation regarding virtues other than justice is more hidden than the nature of obligation regarding justice. And so we do not know the precepts regarding the other virtues as well as we know the precepts regarding acts of justice. And so acts of justice fall specifically within the commandments of the Decalogue, which are the chief elements of the Old Law.

EIGHTH ARTICLE

Can Human Beings Be Dispensed from the Commandments of the Decalogue?

We thus proceed to the eighth inquiry. It seems that human beings can be dispensed from the commandments of the Decalogue, for the following reasons:

Objection 1. The commandments of the Decalogue belong to the natural law. But what is just by nature is wanting in some cases and can be changed, just like human nature, as the Philosopher says in the *Ethics*.[18] But deficiencies of law in particular cases are reasons for dispensing from the law, as I have said before.[19] Therefore, human beings can be dispensed from commandments of the Decalogue.

Obj. 2. As human beings are to the human laws they establish, so is God to the law he establishes. But human beings can dispense from the laws they establish. Therefore, since God established the commandments of the Decalogue, it seems that he can dispense from them. But ecclesiastical superiors take the place of God on earth, for the Apostle says in 2 Cor. 2:10: "For I have also in the person of Christ pardoned what I have pardoned, if anything, for your sakes." Therefore, ecclesiastical superiors also can dispense from the commandments of the Decalogue.

Obj. 3. A prohibition against homicide is included in the commandments of the Decalogue. But human beings seem to dispense from this commandment. For example, the precepts of human law permit human beings such as criminals and enemies to be killed. Therefore, the commandments of the Decalogue can be dispensed.

Obj. 4. Sabbath observance is included in the commandments of the Decalogue. But there was a dispensation regarding this commandment,

---

[18] *Ethics* V, 7 (1134b28–29).   [19] I–II, Q. 96, A. 6; Q. 97, A. 4.

since 1 Mc. 2:41 says: "And they laid plans on that day, saying: 'We shall fight against all those who will come to war against us on the Sabbath.'" Therefore, the commandments of the Decalogue can be dispensed.

On the contrary, Is. 24:5 reproves some because "they have changed the Law and broken the everlasting covenant." But it seems that we should most understand this about the commandments of the Decalogue. Therefore, the commandments of the Decalogue cannot be dispensed.

I answer that, as I have said before,[20] there ought to be dispensations from precepts whenever there arise particular cases in which observance of the letter of the law would be contrary to the intention of the lawmaker. And first and foremost, the intention of any lawmaker is indeed directed to the common good. And second, the intention of a lawmaker is directed to the order of justice and virtue, which preserves and attains the common good. Therefore, if precepts be laid down that include the very preservation of the common good or the very order of justice and virtue, the precepts include the intention of the lawmaker and so cannot be dispensed from. For example, if a community were to have a precept that no one should subvert the commonwealth or betray the political community to its enemies, or that no one should do unjust or evil things, such precepts could not be dispensed from.

But if other precepts subordinate to the latter were to be laid down that specify particular ways to preserve the common good or the order of justice and virtue, such precepts could be dispensed from. The precepts could be dispensed from insofar as their nonobservance in particular cases would not cause prejudice to the first precepts, which include the intention of the lawmaker. For example, if a political community, to preserve the commonwealth, were to decree that citizens stand guard on each street of a besieged city, some citizens could be dispensed for the sake of a greater benefit.

And the commandments of the Decalogue include the very aim of the lawmaker, namely, God. For the commandments of the first tablet, which direct human beings in relation to God, include the very ordination to human beings' common and ultimate good, that is, God. And the commandments of the second tablet include the very ordination of justice to be observed in human society, namely, that nothing improper be done to anyone, and that one should render to others what is their due. For we should so understand the commandments of the Decalogue. And so the commandments of the Decalogue cannot be dispensed from at all.

Reply Obj. 1. The Philosopher is not speaking about the just by nature that includes the very order of justice, since the principle that justice

---

[20] Ibid.

should be observed is never wanting. But he is speaking about specific ways of observing justice, which are wanting in particular cases.

Reply Obj. 2. The Apostle says in 2 Tim. 2:13: "God remains faithful, nor can he deny his very self." But he would deny his very self if he were to remove the very ordination of his justice, since he is justice itself. And so God cannot so dispense human beings that they would be permitted not to be properly related to God, or that they would be permitted not to be subject to the ordination of his justice regarding precepts that direct human beings in their relation to one another.

Reply Obj. 3. The Decalogue prohibits the killing of human beings insofar as such killing has the nature of being undeserved, for then the commandment includes the very nature of justice. And human law cannot make it lawful that human beings be killed undeservedly. But it is not undeserved that criminals and enemies of the commonwealth be killed. And so this is not contrary to the commandment of the Decalogue, nor is such killing murder, which the commandment prohibits, as Augustine says in his work *On Free Choice*.[21] And likewise, it is not theft or robbery, which a commandment of the Decalogue prohibits, if property is taken from one who ought to relinquish it.

And so when the children of Israel at the command of God took away the spoils of the Egyptians,[22] there was no theft, since the spoils were due the Israelites by reason of God's judgment. Likewise, Abraham, when he agreed to kill his son,[23] did not consent to murder, since it was proper that Isaac be killed at the command of God, who is the Lord of life and death. God himself is the one who inflicts death on all human beings, just and unjust, for the sin of our first parent, and human beings will not be murderers if they should by divine authority execute God's judgment, just as God is not a murderer. And likewise, Hosea, having sexual intercourse with a fornicating wife or an adulterous woman,[24] is not an adulterer or fornicator, since he had intercourse with a woman who was his by the command of God, who is the author of the institution of marriage.

Therefore, the commandments of the Decalogue, regarding the nature of justice that they include, cannot be changed. But specifications applying the commandments to particular acts, namely, specifications whether this or that be murder, theft, or adultery, are indeed variable. The specifications sometimes change only because of divine authority, namely, regarding matters that God alone instituted, such as marriage and the like. The specifications also sometimes change because of human authority, as in

[21] *On Free Choice* I, 4, n. 9 (PL 32:1226).   [22] Ex. 12:35–36.   [23] Gen. 22:1–12.   [24] Hos. 1:2–11.

matters committed to the jurisdiction of human beings. For in this but not every respect, human beings take the place of God.

Reply Obj. 4. The cited way of thinking was an interpretation of the commandment rather than a dispensation. For we should not understand that those who do deeds necessary for the human weal violate the Sabbath, as the Lord proves in Mt. 12:3–5.

NINTH ARTICLE

Does the Way of Virtue Fall under Command of the Law?

We thus proceed to the ninth inquiry. It seems that the way of virtue does fall under command of the law, for the following reasons:

Objection 1. The way of virtue consists of persons doing just deeds justly, and brave deeds bravely, and the like regarding other virtues. But Dt. 16:20 commands: "You shall carry out just deeds justly." Therefore, the way of virtue falls under command of the law.

Obj. 2. What belongs to the lawmaker's intention falls most under the law's command. But the lawmaker chiefly aims to make human beings virtuous, as the *Ethics* says.[25] And it belongs to the virtuous to act virtuously. Therefore, the way of virtue falls under command of the law.

Obj. 3. Properly speaking, the way of virtue seems to consist of acting willingly and with pleasure. But this falls under command of the divine law, for Ps. 100:2 says: "Serve the Lord in gladness," and 2 Cor. 9:7 says: "Do not act out of sadness or necessity, for the Lord loves a cheerful giver." And a gloss on the latter says: "Do cheerfully the good you do, and then you act well. But if you act with sadness, the good is done from you, not by you."[26] Therefore, the way of virtue falls under command of the law.

On the contrary, one can act in a virtuous way only if one should possess a virtuous habit, as the Philosopher makes clear in the *Ethics*.[27] But anyone transgressing the command of a law deserves punishment. Therefore, if the way of virtue falls under command of the law, one without a virtuous habit would deserve punishment no matter what he or she does. But this is contrary to the aim of the law, which strives to induce human beings to virtue by habituating them to good deeds. Therefore, the way of virtue does not fall under command of the law.

I answer that commands of the law have the power to compel compliance, as I have said before.[28] Therefore, what the law compels falls directly

---

25 Aristotle, *Ethics* II, 1 (1103b3–6). [26]*Glossa ordinaria*, on 2 Cor. 9:17 (PL 114:564); Peter Lombard, *Glossa*, on 2 Cor. 9:17 (PL 192:63). [27]*Ethics* II, 4 (1105a17–21); V, 8 (1135b24). [28]I–II, Q. 90, A. 3, *ad* 2.

under command of the law. And the law compels compliance by fear of punishment, as the *Ethics* says,[29] since that for which legal punishment is inflicted falls strictly under command of the law. And the divine law and human law are differently disposed in regard to ordaining punishment. For legal punishment is inflicted only for things regarding which lawmakers have the power to judge, since the law punishes by passing sentence. And human beings, who lay down human laws, have the power to judge only regarding external acts, since "human beings perceive sensibly perceptible things," as 1 Sam. 16:7 says. But only God, who lays down the divine law, has the power to judge regarding interior movements of the will, as Ps. 7:9 says: "God scrutinizes our desires and emotions."

Therefore, we should accordingly say that both divine law and human law concern the way of virtue in one respect, that the divine law but not human law concerns the way of virtue in another respect, and that neither the divine law nor human law concerns the way of virtue in a third respect.

And the way of virtue consists of three things, as the Philosopher says in the *Ethics*.[30] And the first of these is whether one acts knowingly. And both the divine law and human law judge this, since one does accidentally what one does unknowingly. And so both the divine law and human law deem deeds worthy of punishment or pardon depending on the person's knowledge or ignorance.

The second consideration is whether one acts willingly, that is, by choice and by choosing to do something for its own sake. And we thereby signify two interior movements, namely, of willing and intending, about which I have spoken before.[31] And only the divine law, not human law, judges these two interior movements. For human law does not punish one who wants to kill and does not, but the divine law does, as Mt. 5:22 says: "Those who are angry with their brother will be liable to judgment."

And the third consideration is whether one has the power to act firmly and consistently and does so. And such firmness, properly speaking, belongs to habits, namely, that one act by reason of ingrained habit. And in this respect, the way of virtue does not fall under command of the law, whether the divine law or human law. For example, neither human beings nor God punish as trangressors of the law those who give requisite honor to their parents but do not have the habit of filial piety.

Reply Obj. 1. The way one performs just acts falling under command of the law is that the deeds be done according to the ordination of the law, not that they be done by reason of the habit of justice.

---

[29] Aristotle, *Ethics* X, 9 (1179b11–18). [30] Ibid. II, 4 (1105a31–b5). [31] I–II, QQ. 8, 12.

Reply Obj. 2. The intention of a lawmaker concerns two things. One is indeed what lawmakers strive to induce by legal commands, and this is virtue. And the second is what lawmakers intend legal commands to impose, and this is what leads or disposes citizens to virtue, that is, virtuous acts. For the end of precepts, and what precepts lay down, are not the same thing, just as ends and means are not the same in regard to other things.

Reply Obj. 3. It falls under a command of the divine law that we perform virtuous acts unbegrudgingly, since those who act begrudgingly act unwillingly. And to act with pleasure, that is, joyfully or cheerfully, falls under the command of the law in one respect, namely, insofar as pleasure results from love of God and neighbor, which falls under the command of the law. But to act with pleasure does not fall under the command of the law in another respect, namely, insofar as habits result in pleasure, since "pleasure in deeds is evidence that persons have become habituated," as the *Ethics* says.[32] For acts can be pleasurable either because of their end or because of suitable habits.

TENTH ARTICLE
Does the Way of Charity Fall under Command of the Divine Law?

We thus proceed to the tenth inquiry. It seems that the way of charity does fall under command of the divine law, for the following reasons:

Objection 1. Mt. 19:17 says: "If you wish to enter into life, keep the commandments." And it seems from this that keeping the commandments suffices to lead human beings into life. But good deeds do not suffice to lead human beings into life unless the deeds are done out of charity. For 1 Cor. 13:3 says: "If I have distributed all my goods to feed the poor, and if I have delivered my body to be burned, it profits me nothing if I should not have charity." Therefore, the way of charity is included in what the law commands.

Obj. 2. It belongs strictly to the way of charity that everything be done for God. But this falls under command of the law, for the Apostle says in 1 Cor. 10:31: "Do everything for the glory of God." Therefore, the way of charity falls under command of the law.

Obj. 3. If the way of charity does not fall under command of the law, then one can fulfill commands of the law without possessing charity. But what can be done without charity can be done without grace, which always accompanies charity. Therefore, one can fulfill commands of the

---

[32] Aristotle, *Ethics* II, 3 (1104b3–9).

law without grace. But this is the error of Pelagius, as Augustine makes clear in his work *On Heresies*.[33] Therefore, the way of charity is included in what the law commands.

On the contrary, those who do not keep the commands of the law commit mortal sin. Therefore, if the way of charity falls under command of the law, then those who do anything otherwise than out of charity commit mortal sin. But those who do not possess charity do not act out of charity. Therefore, those who do not possess charity commit mortal sins in their every deed, however good the deed is by its nature. But this conclusion is improper.

I answer that there have been conflicting views on this matter. For example, some have said that the way of charity is absolutely under command of the law.[34] Nor is it impossible to keep this command if one does not possess charity, since such people can dispose themselves so that God infuses charity in them. Nor does a person commit mortal sin whenever the person does something by its nature good, since the command that one act out of charity is an affirmative precept and morally obliges only when one possesses charity, not at all times. And others have said that the way of charity does not at all fall under command of the law.

And both of these opinions are true in some respect. For we can consider acts of charity in two ways. We can consider them in one way insofar as they are acts of charity as such. And they in this respect fall under commands of the law that lay down specific commands (e.g., "Thou shalt love the Lord thy God,"[35] and "Thou shalt love thy neighbor"[36]). And the first opinion is true in this respect. For it is not impossible to observe these precepts, which concern acts of charity, since human beings can dispose themselves to possess charity and can exercise charity after they have possessed it.

We can consider acts of charity in a second way insofar as they are the way of acts of other virtues, that is, as acts of other virtues are ordained to charity, which is "the purpose of commands," as 1 Tim. 1:5 says. For I have said before that the intended end is a formal modality of acts ordained for the end.[37] And the second opinion, that the way of charity does not fall under the command of the law, is true in this respect, that is to say, that the commandment "Honor thy father"[38] only commands that one honor one's father, not that one honor one's father out of charity. And so those who honor their fathers, even if they do not possess charity, do not become transgressors of the precept to honor one's father, although

---

[33] *On Heresies* 88 (PL 42:47–48).   [34] E.g., Albert the Great, *Commentary on the Sentences* III, dist. 36, a. 6.   [35] Dt. 6:5.   [36] Lev. 19:18.   [37] I–II, Q. 12: A. 1, *ad* 3; A. 4, *ad* 3.   [38] Ex. 20:12; Dt. 5:16.

they are transgressors of the precept regarding acts of charity. And they deserve punishment because of the latter transgression.

Reply Obj. 1. The Lord said: "If you wish to enter into life, keep all the commandments," not: "If you wish to enter into life, keep one commandment." And the commandment to love God and neighbor is included in the commandments.

Reply Obj. 2. That one love God with one's whole heart is included in the commandment of charity, to which commandment it belongs to relate everything to God. And so human beings can fulfill the precept of charity only by relating everything to God. Therefore, those honoring their parents are morally obliged to do so out of charity by force of the commandment "Thou shalt love the Lord thy God with all thy heart,"[39] not by force of the commandment "Honor thy parents."[40] And since these are two commandments that do not oblige at all times, they can oblige at different times. And so one may fulfill the precept about honoring one's parents without transgressing the precept about omitting the way of charity.

Reply Obj. 3. Human beings cannot keep all the commandments of the law unless they fulfill the precept of charity, which is not done without grace. And so what Pelagius said, that human beings fulfill the law without grace, is impossible.

ELEVENTH ARTICLE
Do We Appropriately Mark Out Other Moral Precepts of the Law besides the Decalogue?

We thus proceed to the eleventh inquiry. It seems that we do not appropriately mark out other moral precepts of the Law besides the Decalogue, for the following reasons:

Objection 1. The Lord says in Mt. 22:40: "The whole law and the prophets depend on the two precepts of love." But the Ten Commandments explain these two precepts. Therefore, there need not be other moral precepts.

Obj. 2. We distinguish moral precepts from ceremonial precepts and precepts governing the administration of justice, as I have said.[41] But specifying general moral precepts belongs to ceremonial precepts and precepts governing the administration of justice, and general moral precepts are included in, or even presupposed by, the Decalogue, as I have said.[42] Therefore, it is inappropriate that there be other moral precepts besides the Decalogue.

---

[39]Dt. 6:5.　　[40]Ex. 20:12; Dt. 5:6.　　[41]I–II, Q. 99, A. 3.　　[42]A. 3.

Obj. 3. Moral precepts concern every kind of virtuous act, as I have said before.[43] Therefore, as the Old Law lays down moral precepts pertaining to worship, generosity, mercy, and chastity, in addition to the Decalogue, so also should the Old Law have laid down precepts pertaining to other virtues (e.g., courage, sobriety, and the like). But we do not find such in the Old Law. Therefore, we do not appropriately mark out in the Old Law other moral precepts besides the Decalogue.

On the contrary, Ps. 19:8 says: "The law of the Lord is spotless, converting souls." But other moral precepts added to the Decalogue also preserve human beings from the stain of sin and convert their souls to God. Therefore, it also belonged to the Old Law to lay down other moral precepts.

I answer that, as is clear from what I have said before,[44] ceremonial precepts and precepts governing the administration of justice derive their force only from their institution, since it did not seem to matter whether things should be done in this way or that before the precepts were instituted. But moral precepts have efficacy from the very dictates of natural reason even if the precepts were never laid down in the Old Law. And there are three classes of moral precepts. For some moral precepts are most certain and so evident to reason that they need no promulgation. For example, such are the commandments to love God and neighbor, and the like, as I have said before,[45] and these commandments are the ends of the commandments, as it were. And so no one's reason can judge erroneously about them. And some moral precepts are more specific, and everyone, even ordinary people, can at once easily perceive their reasonableness. And yet they need to be promulgated, since human reason in a few instances may be led astray regarding them. And such are the commandments of the Decalogue. And there are some moral precepts whose reasonableness is evident only to the wise but not so evident to everyone. And these are the moral precepts added to the Decalogue, precepts laid down by God for the people through Moses and Aaron.

But because evident things are the sources for knowing things that are not evident, we trace the moral precepts added to the Decalogue to the commandments of the Decalogue as corollaries. For example, the First Commandment of the Decalogue[46] prohibits worship of strange gods, and

---

[43] A. 2.   [44] I–II, Q. 99, A. 3.   [45] A. 3; A. 4, *ad* 1.   [46] Thomas Aquinas follows the Vulgate numbering and division of the commandments. What the Vulgate enumerates as the First Commandment, the King James Version enumerates as the First and Second Commandments; and what the Vulgate enumerates as the Ninth and Tenth Commandments, the King James Version enumerates as the Tenth Commandment.

precepts are added thereto prohibiting things ordained for the worship of idols. Thus Dt. 18:10 relates: "Let there be among you none who would purify their sons and daughters by fire, nor let there be any wizard or witch, nor let anyone consult fortune-tellers or diviners, nor let anyone seek truth from the dead."

And the Second Commandment prohibits perjury. And Lev. 24:15–16 adds a prohibition of blasphemy thereto, and Dt. 13:1–11 adds a prohibition of false teaching.

And all the ceremonial precepts are added to the Third Commandment.

And the precept about honoring the elderly, as Lev. 19:32 says, "Rise in the presence of a hoary head, and honor the person of the elderly," is added to the Fourth Commandment about honoring one's parents. And more generally, all the precepts prescribing that we show respect to our betters and kindness to our equals or inferiors are added to that commandment.

And there is a prohibition of hate or any violence against our neighbor, as Lev. 19:16 says, "You shall not stand against the blood of your neighbor," and there is also a prohibition of hatred of one's brother, as Lev. 19:17 says, "You shall not hate your brother in your heart." These prohibitions are added to the Fifth Commandment, which concerns the prohibition of murder.

And there is a precept prohibiting prostitution, as Dt. 23:17 says, "There will be no prostitute among the daughters of Israel nor whoremonger among the sons of Israel," and there is also a precept prohibiting the sin against nature, as Lev. 18:22–23 says, "You shall not have sexual intercourse with a fellow male or any beast." These precepts are added to the Sixth Commandment, which concerns the prohibition of adultery.

And there is a precept prohibiting interest-taking, as Dt. 23:19 says, "You shall not lend to your brother at interest," and there is a prohibition against fraud, as Dt. 25:13 says, "You shall not put different weights in your sack." And more generally, there are all the precepts that pertain to prohibiting trickery and robbery. These precepts are added to the Seventh Commandment, which prohibits theft.

And there is a prohibition against passing false judgment, as Ex. 23:2 says, "Nor shall you depart from the truth by yielding to the judgment of the majority," and there is a prohibition of lying, as Ex. 23:7 says, "You shall avoid lying." And there is a prohibition of detraction, as Lev. 19:16 says, "You shall not be a detractor or scandalmonger among the people." These prohibitions are added to the Eighth Commandment, which concerns the prohibition of false testimony.

And no other precepts are added to the last two commandments, since these commandments prohibit all evil coveting without exception.

Reply Obj. 1. The commandments of the Decalogue are directed to the love of God and neighbor by reason of the clear nature of the obligations, but other precepts are so directed by reason of their less evident nature.

Reply Obj. 2. Ceremonial precepts and precepts governing the administration of justice specify commandments of the Decalogue by force of the precepts' institution and not by force of an inclination from nature, as the additional moral precepts do.

Reply Obj. 3. Legal precepts are ordained for the common good, as I have said before.[47] And virtues directing us in relation to others pertain directly to the common good, and likewise the virtue of chastity, inasmuch as the reproductive act promotes the common good of the species. Therefore, the commandments of the Decalogue and the precepts added thereto are laid down regarding those virtues. And regarding acts of courage, commanders exhorting troops in a war undertaken for the common good give the troops commands, as Dt. 20:3 makes clear when priests are commanded to say: "Do not be afraid, do not retreat." Likewise, the prohibition of acts of gluttony is committed to paternal admonition, since such acts are contrary to the good of the household. And so Dt. 21:20 says in the person of parents: "He contemns listening to our admonitions, he wastes himself in extravagances and lusts and feasting."

TWELFTH ARTICLE
Did the Moral Precepts of the Old Law Make Human Beings Just?

We thus proceed to the twelfth inquiry. It seems that the moral precepts of the Old Law made human beings just, for the following reasons:

Objection 1. The Apostle says in Rom. 2:13: "For those who observe the Law will be made just, and those who merely listen to the Law have not been." But we call those who fulfill the precepts of the Law observers of the Law. Therefore, fulfilling the precepts of the Law made human beings just.

Obj. 2. Lev. 18:5 says: "Keep my laws and judgments, and human beings, if they do so, will thereby have life." But human beings have spiritual life by being just. Therefore, fulfilling the precepts of the Law made human beings just.

Obj. 3. The divine law is more efficacious than human law. But human law makes human beings just, since there is a justice in fulfilling precepts of that law. Therefore, precepts of the Law made human beings just.

---

[47]I–II, Q. 90, A. 2.

On the contrary, the Apostle says in 2 Cor. 3:6: "The letter of the Law kills." But as Augustine says in his work *On the Spirit and Letter of the Law,*[48] we also understand the statement of the Apostle to refer to the moral precepts of the Law. Therefore, the moral precepts of the Old Law did not make human beings just.

I answer that we properly and primarily predicate health of what possesses health, and secondarily of what signifies or preserves health. Just so, we primarily and properly predicate justification of the very process that makes human beings just, and we can secondarily and improperly, as it were, predicate justification of what signifies justice or disposes to justice. And the precepts of the Old Law evidently made human beings just in the latter two respects, namely, inasmuch as the precepts disposed human beings to the justifying grace of Christ, and the precepts also signified that grace. This is so because, as Augustine says in his work *Against Faustus,*[49] "the life of that people foretold and prefigured Christ."

But if we should speak of justification in the strict sense, then we need to note that we can understand justice as habitual or actual, and we accordingly speak of justification in two ways. We indeed speak of justification in one way as human beings who acquire the habit of justice become just. And we speak of justification in a second way as human beings perform just deeds, so that justification in this respect is simply the execution of justice. And we can understand justice, like other virtues, as either acquired or infused, as is evident from what I have said before.[50] And deeds indeed produce the acquired virtue of justice, but God himself by infusing his grace produces the infused virtue of justice. And the latter justice is the true justice about which we are now speaking, regarding which one is called just with God, as Rom. 4:2 says: "If works of the Law made Abraham just, he has reason to boast, but not with God." Therefore, the moral precepts of the Old Law, which concern human acts, could not produce such justice. And so the moral precepts could not make human beings just by producing such justice.

And if we should understand justification to mean the execution of justice, then all the precepts of the Old Law made human beings just in one way or another. For example, the ceremonial precepts in general indeed included justice as such, namely, insofar as they were observed for the worship of God, although those precepts in particular included justice as such only because the divine law so specified. And so we say that such precepts made human beings just only by the devotion or the obedience of those carrying out the precepts.

---

[48] *On the Spirit and Letter of the Law* 14 (PL 44:215).   [49] *Against Faustus* XXII, 24 (PL 42:417).   [50] I–II, Q. 63, A. 4.

And the moral precepts and the precepts governing the administration of justice, either in general or in particular, included matter pertaining to justice as such. And the moral precepts included matter pertaining to justice as such regarding general justice, that is, "all virtue," as the *Ethics* says.[51] And the precepts governing the administration of justice pertain to particular justice, which concerns the interactions of human life, which transpire among human beings in their relations to one another.

Reply Obj. 1. The Apostle in the cited text understands justification to mean the execution of justice.

Reply Obj. 2. The cited text says that the human beings who fulfilled the precepts of the Law had life thereby in that they did not incur the penalty of death that the Law inflicted on transgressors. And the Apostle in Gal. 3:12 quotes the passage in this sense.

Reply Obj. 3. The precepts of human law make human beings just by acquired justice, and we are presently speaking only about justice with God, not about acquired justice.

---

[51] Aristotle, *Ethics* V, 1 (1129b30–31).

QUESTION 105

On the Reason for Precepts Governing
the Administration of Justice

FIRST ARTICLE
Did the Old Law Ordain Fitting Precepts Regarding Rulers?

We thus proceed to the first inquiry. It seems that the Old Law did not ordain fitting precepts regarding rulers, for the following reasons:

Objection 1. "The right order of the people depends chiefly on the chief ruler," as the Philosopher says in the *Politics.*[1] But we do not find in the Law how the supreme ruler ought to be established, although we find prescriptions regarding inferior officials. First, indeed, we find the prescription in Ex. 18:21–22: "Provide wise men from all the people," etc. And we find the prescription in Num. 11:16–17: "Gather for me seventy men from the elders of Israel," etc. And we find the prescription in Dt. 1:13–18: "Give me wise and knowledgeable men from among you," etc. Therefore, the Old Law inadequately ordained rulers of the people.

Obj. 2. "It belongs to the best to lead to the best things," as Plato says.[2] But the best regime of a political community or any people is to be governed by a king, since such a regime most represents the divine regime, in which God governs the world from its beginning. Therefore, the Law should have established a king for the people and not have left this to their choice, as Dt. 17:14–16 permits: "When you shall say, 'I shall establish a king over me,' you shall establish him," etc.

Obj. 3. Mt. 12:25 says: "Every kingdom divided against itself shall be laid low." And this was also evidenced by trial and error in the history of the Jewish people, regarding whom the division of the kingdom brought about its destruction. But law should chiefly aim at things pertaining to the commonweal of the people. Therefore, the Law should have prohibited division of the kingdom under two kings. Nor should even divine authority have introduced such a division, since we read in 1 Kgs. 11:29–31 that it was introduced by the authority of the prophet Ahijah of Shiloh.

Obj. 4. As priests are instituted for the benefit of the people regarding things that pertain to God, as Heb. 5:1 makes clear, so also rulers are instituted for the benefit of the people regarding human affairs. But cer-

---

[1] *Politics* III, 4 (1278b8–10).   [2] Cf. *Timaeus* 29A; 29E.

tain things (c.g., tithes and first fruits and many other like things) were allotted to the priests and Levites of the Old Law as a means of their livelihood. Therefore, certain things should likewise have been ordained for the rulers of the people to provide them with a livelihood. And this is especially so because the rulers were prohibited from accepting bribes, as Ex. 23:8 makes clear: "You shall not take bribes, which blind even the wise and pervert the responses of the just."

Obj. 5. As a kingdom is the best regime, so tyranny is the most corrupt regime. But the Lord by establishing a king established tyrannical law, for 1 Sam. 8:11–17 says: "This will be the law of the king who will reign over you: he will take away your sons," etc. Therefore, the Old Law made inappropriate provision regarding the institution of rulers.

On the contrary, Num. 24:5 commends the people of Israel for the beauty of its institutions: "How beautiful are your tabernacles, O Jacob, and your tents, O Israel." But the beauty of the institutions of a people depends on the right institution of its rulers. Therefore, the Old Law made the right institution for the people regarding its rulers.

I answer that we should note two things regarding the right institution of rulers in any political community or people. The first is that all citizens should participate in the regime, since this maintains civic peace, and since all citizens love and protect such an institution, as the *Politics* says.[3] The second is what we note regarding types of regimes, that is, forms of government. And although regimes have different forms, as the Philosopher notes in the *Politics*,[4] the chief forms are a kingdom, in which one person rules by reason of the person's virtue, and aristocracy (i.e., government by the best), in which a few persons rule by reason of their virtue. And so the best institution of rulers belongs to a city or kingdom in which one person is chosen by reason of his virtue to rule over all, and other persons govern under him by reason of their virtue. And yet such a regime belongs to all citizens, both because its rulers are chosen from the citizens, and because all citizens choose its rulers. For this is the best constitution, a happy mixture of kingdom, since one person rules, and aristocracy, since many govern by reason of their virtue, and democracy (i.e., government by the people), since rulers can be chosen from the people, and since the choice of rulers belongs to the people.

And the divine law established such a regime. For Moses and his successors governed the people, individually ruling over all, as it were, and this regime is a form of kingdom. And seventy-two elders were chosen by

---

[3] Aristotle, *Politics* II, 6 (1270b17–19).   [4] Ibid. III, 5 (1279a32–b10).

reason of their virtue, for Dt. 1:15 says: "I took wise and honorable men from your tribes and constituted them rulers." And this was aristocratic. And the regime was democratic in that the rulers were chosen from all the people, for Ex. 18:21 says: "Provide wise men from all the people," etc., and in that the people chose the rulers, and so Dt. 1:13 says: "Take wise men from among you," etc. And so the best institution of rulers was the one that the Old Law established.

Reply Obj. 1. The people were ruled under the special care of God, and so Dt. 7:6 says: "The Lord your God chose you to be a special people." And so God reserved to himself the institution of the chief ruler. And Num. 27:16 relates that Moses sought this: "Let the Lord God of the spirits of all flesh provide a man to rule this people." And so the ordination of God established Joshua to rule after Moses. And we read about particular judges who succeeded Joshua, as Jgs. 3:9–10, 15 makes clear, that God "raised up a savior for the people," and that "the spirit of God was in them." And so the Lord did not commit the choice of a king to the people. Rather, he reserved the choice to himself, as Dt. 17:15 says: "You shall constitute as king the one the Lord your God has chosen."

Reply Obj. 2. A kingdom, if it be not corrupted, is the best regime for the people. But a kingdom easily degenerates into tyranny because of the great power granted a king, unless the one granted such power should have complete virtue. For it belongs only to the virtuous to bear themselves well when favored by good fortune, as the Philosopher says in the *Ethics*.[5] And few persons have complete virtue, and the Jews were particularly cruel and prone to avarice, through which vices human beings most fall into tyranny. And so the Lord at the beginning did not establish a king with complete power over the people but established judges and governors to protect them. But he, almost indignantly, granted the people a king when they petitioned for one, as 1 Sam. 8:7 makes clear by what he said to Samuel: "They have not rejected you but me, that I not rule over them."

Nonetheless, he from the beginning established regarding the institution of kingship, indeed first of all, the means of choosing a king. And he established two things in this regard, namely, that they await the judgment of the Lord in choosing a king, and that they not make a foreigner king, since such kings are usually little attached to the people over whom they are appointed, and so do not care about them.

Second, he ordained regarding kings when established how they should conduct themselves regarding themselves, namely, that they not

---

[5] *Ethics* IV, 3 (1124a30–b4).

have many horses or wives or immense riches, since rulers descend to tyranny and abandon justice by coveting such things.

Third, he established how they should dispose themselves toward God, namely, that they should always read and meditate on God's Law and always fear and obey God.

Fourth, he established how they should dispose themselves toward their subjects, namely, that they not in their pride contemn or oppress their subjects, and that they not deviate from justice.

Reply Obj. 3. The division of the kingdom and plurality of kings was inflicted on the people as punishment for their many rebellions, which they especially undertook against the just David, rather than for their benefit. And so Hos. 13:11 says: "In my wrath, I shall give you a king." And Hos. 8:4 says: "They reigned, but not by my will; rulers appeared, and I did not know them."

Reply Obj. 4. Priests were appointed to perform the sacred ministry by successive generations from father to son. And this was done so that they be held in greater respect if not anyone of the people could become a priest, since the honor they received added to respect for the divine worship. And so special things, both in tithes and first fruits and regarding oblations and sacrifices, needed to be allotted to them as the means of their livelihood. But rulers were taken from the whole people, as I have said, and so they had fixed possessions of their own as the means of their livelihood, and especially since the Lord also prohibited kings from having excessive wealth or displaying magnificence. The Lord prohibited these things both because it was difficult not to be incited by them to pride and tyranny, and because common people did not usually strive for them if the rulers were not very rich, and if the rulers' office was laborious and full of anxiety. And so the occasion for sedition was removed.

Reply Obj. 5. The divine institution of kingship did not give to the kings of Israel any right to make tyrannical law. Rather, the Lord foretold that the kings of Israel, who, degenerating into tyranny and preying on their subjects, made evil laws to suit themselves, would claim a right to make such laws. And 1 Sam. 8:17 makes this clear: "And you will be the king's slaves," which belongs strictly to tyranny in that tyrants rule over their subjects as if their subjects were their slaves. And so Samuel said this to deter the people from seeking a king, for a subsequent verse, v. 19, says: "The people would not listen to the voice of Samuel."

But a good king may without tyranny have occasion to take sons away and constitute them tribunes or centurions, and to take many things from his subjects, in order to secure the common good.

GLOSSARY

Action: *activity*. There are two basic kinds of activity. One kind, transitive activity, is efficient causality, that is, action that produces an effect in something else. Thomas Aquinas usually uses the word *action* in connection with transitive action. The second kind, immanent action, perfects only the being that acts. Immanent action produces effects in living finite beings. Plants have the immanent activities of nutrition, growth, and reproduction. Animals have, in addition, the immanent activities of sense perception and sense appetites. Human beings have, in addition, immanent activities of the intellect and the will. *See* Cause.

Appetite: *the desire or striving of finite beings to actualize potentialities*. Nonliving material beings have natural appetites. Plants have, in addition, the vegetative appetites of nutrition, growth, and reproduction. Animals have, in addition, sense appetites. Human beings have, in addition, an intellectual or rational appetite, the will. *See* Concupiscible, Irascible, Will.

Cause: *something that contributes to the being or coming-to-be of something else*. The term refers primarily to an efficient cause, that is, a cause that by its activity produces an effect. For example, a builder and those who work under the builder are efficient causes of the house they are building. A final cause is the end for the sake of which an efficient cause acts. For example, a builder builds a house to provide a dwelling suitable for human habitation (objective purpose) and to make money if the house is to be sold (subjective purpose). An exemplary cause is the idea or model of a desired effect in the mind of an intellectual efficient cause that preconceives the effect. For example, a builder preconceives the form of the house he or she intends to build. Efficient, final, and exemplary causes are extrinsic to the effects they produce. In addition, form, which makes an effect to be what it is, and matter, which receives the form, are correlative intrinsic causes. For example, houses are composed of bricks and mortar (the matter), which are given a structure or shape (the form). *See* End, Form, Intention, Matter.

Charity: *the supernatural virtue whereby one is characteristically disposed to love God above all things and to love all other things for his sake. See* Virtue.

Concupiscence: *the inclination of human beings' sense appetites toward actions contrary to the ordination of reason, with the inclination not being completely subject to control by reason*. Concupiscence is not to be identified with the concupiscible appetites as such. *See* Concupiscible, Will.

Concupiscible: *a sense appetite for something pleasant*. Love and hate, desire and aversion, joy and sorrow are movements of concupiscible appetites. *See* Appetite, Irascible.

Conscience: *the dictate of reason that one should or should not do something. See* Synderesis.

Emotions: *movements of sense appetites.* Emotions may be ordinate (in accord with right reason) or inordinate (contrary to right reason). Emotions involve either desire for pleasant things or repugnance regarding difficult things. *See* Concupiscible, Irascible, Moral Virtues.

End: *the object for the sake of which something acts.* The end may be intrinsic or extrinsic. The end is intrinsic if it belongs to the nature of an active thing. The end is extrinsic if it is the conscious object of a rational being's action. *See* Cause.

Essence: *that which makes things what they substantially are.* For example, the human essence makes human beings to be what they are as substances, namely, rational animals. When the essence of a being is considered as the ultimate source of the being's activities and development, it is called the being's nature. For example, human nature is the ultimate source of specifically human activities (activities of reason and activities according to reason). *See* Form.

Form: *that which makes things to be the kind of thing they are or to possess additional attributes.* For example, the human form makes human beings human, and other forms make them so tall and so heavy. *See* Essence, Matter.

Habit: *the characteristic disposition or inclination to be or to act in a certain way.* Habits belong chiefly to the soul, that is, to the intellect and the will. They may be innate or acquired, natural or supernatural, good or bad. For example, the habit of logical argumentation belongs to the intellect; the habit of moderation belongs to the will; the habits of the first principles of theoretical and practical reason are innate; the habit of cleanliness is acquired; the habit of courage is natural; the habit of faith is supernatural; the habit of generosity is good; the habit of stinginess is bad. Habits belong secondarily, not chiefly, to the body, as the latter is disposed or made apt to be readily at the service of the soul's activity. *See* Virtue.

Intellect: *the human faculty of understanding, judging, and reasoning.* Thomas Aquinas, following Aristotle, holds that there is an active power of the intellect that moves the passive or potential power of the intellect to understand the essence of material things, to form judgments, and to reason deductively. *See* Reason.

Intention: *striving for things.* Human beings, who have the power of reason, desire things knowingly and rationally. Irrational animals, which have cognitive sense powers but no power of reason, desire things knowingly but not rationally. Other material things, which have natural appetites but no cognitive power, strive for things unknowingly. *See* Appetite, Cause, End.

Irascible: *a sense appetite for a useful object that can be attained only with difficulty.* The object does not seem pleasant and can be attained only by overcoming opposition. Hope and despair, fear and anger are movements of irascible appetites. *See* Appetite, Concupiscible.

Justice: *the moral virtue consisting of the right characteristic disposition of the will to render to others what is due them.* This is the special virtue of justice, and there are two particular kinds. One kind, commutative justice, concerns the duties of individuals and groups to other individuals and groups. The other kind, distributive justice, concerns the duties of the community to insure that individuals and groups receive a share of the community's goods proportional to the individuals' and groups' contributions to the community. But justice in general is moral virtue in general, insofar as all moral virtues can be directed to the common good. Thomas calls such justice legal justice because human laws prescribe the moral virtues expected of citizens. *See* Moral Virtues, Virtue.

Law: *an ordination or order of reason, for the common good, by one with authority, and promulgated.* For Thomas Aquinas, the archetypical law is God's plan for the universe and everything he creates. Aquinas calls this plan the eternal law. Human beings, as rational creatures, can understand God's plan for them and can judge what behavior it requires for them, and they in this way participate in the eternal law. Aquinas calls this participation in the eternal law the natural law. And human beings need to establish laws for their communities. These human laws either adopt conclusions from the general precepts of the natural law (for example, do not commit murder) or further specify the precepts (for example, drive on the right side of the road). Aquinas calls those human laws that are proximate conclusions from the general precepts of the natural law the common law of peoples (*jus gentium*), and he calls those human laws that are more remote conclusions from, or further specifications of, the general precepts civil laws.

Matter: *the stuff or subject matter out of which things are constituted. See* Cause, Form.

Moral Virtues: *virtues consisting of the right characteristic disposition of the will toward requisite ends (for example, just, courageous, moderate deeds).* Reason directs moral virtues, theoretical reason by understanding their ends, and practical wisdom by choosing means to those ends. Moral virtues concern the mean between too much and too little. One moral virtue, justice, concerns external things. Other moral virtues concern control of emotions. *See* Emotions, Justice, Practical Wisdom.

Nature: *see* Essence.

Political Community: *the organized community wherein and whereby human beings are able fully to achieve their proper excellence or well-being.* Like Aristotle, Thomas Aquinas holds that human beings are by their nature social and political animals. Human beings need to associate with one another for self-defense and economic development, but they also and especially need to associate with one another for their full intellectual and moral development. Only an organized community of a certain size can be self-sufficient to achieve these goals. Political community thus differs from the state, which is the supreme agency responsible for organizing the community, and differs from government, which is the machinery and personnel of the state. Unlike Aristotle, however, Aquinas envisioned a supernatural end for human beings beyond their temporal well-being, and by reason of that the supernatural end, the membership of Christians in another, divinely established community, the church. The relation between the natural and the supernatural ends of human beings, and the relation between the two communities promoting those ends, were important concerns of Aquinas. *See* Polity.

Polity: *the regime or constitution that gives a political community its distinctive form.* For Thomas Aquinas, polity also has the meaning of a particular regime or constitution that mixes or combines elements of rule that is monarchic (rule by one best person), aristocratic (rule by the few best persons), and democratic (rule by the multitude). Such a regime includes only limited popular participation. *See* Political Community.

Power: *the active capacity to perform a certain kind of activity.* For example, the intellect and the will are powers of human beings.

Practical Wisdom (Prudence): *the intellectual virtue consisting of the right charcteristic disposition to reason about what human beings should or should not do.* Practical wisdom concerns human action and so differs from theoretical wisdom, which concerns the ultimate causes of things irrespective of related human action. Theoretical reason understands the ends of moral virtues, and practical wisdom chooses the means to those ends. As the most important natural virtue connected with human action, practical wisdom is sometimes considered as if it were one of the moral virtues. *See* Habit, Moral Virtues, Virtue.

Principle: *the universal major premise of an argument.* Principles presupposing no principle, or at least no principle other than the principle of contradiction, are called first principles. There are theoretical first principles (for example, everything coming to be has a cause) and practical first principles (for example, do good, avoid evil, live sociably with others).

Reason: *(1) the process of drawing conclusions from principles; (2) the power to draw conclusions from principles; (3) the power of the intellect in general.* In the selections in this work, Thomas Aquinas frequently uses the term in the third sense. *See* Intellect.

Regime: *see* Polity.

Slavery: *involuntary servitude.* In medieval society, war captives became slaves, and their servitude could be terminated only by ransom or treaty. The feudal institutions of serfdom and vassalage were similar to slavery in that serfs, vassals,

and their children were bound to certain lifetime duties to their lords and masters. But serfs and vassals, unlike the slaves of ancient Greece and Rome and
those of the antebellum American South, had rights that their lords and masters
were theoretically bound to respect.

Subject: *a human being bound to obey another human being.* For example, British
citizens are British subjects, that is, bound to obey British authorities.

Synderesis: habitual understanding of the first principles governing human action.
This is an innate disposition. Human beings are disposed by their rational nature
to recognize that they should seek the good proper to their human nature and
should avoid things contrary to it. The human good involves preserving one's life
in reasonable ways, mating and raising offspring in reasonable ways, seeking
truth, and living cooperatively with others in an organized society. *See* Habit.

Virtue: *human excellence.* Virtue is a perduring quality and so a characteristic
disposition. Thomas Aquinas distinguishes three kinds of virtue: intellectual,
moral, and theological. Intellectual virtues have intellectual activities as their
object. Concerning theoretical truth, intellectual virtues comprise understanding
first principles, scientific knowledge, and theoretical wisdom. Concerning practical truth, intellectual virtues comprise practical wisdom and skills. Moral virtues
consist of characteristic readiness to act in practical matters as practical wisdom
dictates. Practical wisdom and moral virtues may be acquired or infused. There
are three infused theological virtues: faith, hope, and charity. *See* Charity, Habit,
Moral Virtues, Practical Wisdom, Principle.

Will: *human beings' intellectual (rational) appetite, the intellectual faculty of desire.*
The will necessarily desires the ultimate human perfection, happiness, but freely
desires particular goods, since the latter are only partially good.

SELECT BIBLIOGRAPHY

On Aristotle's philosophical system, see:

Ackrill, J.L., *Aristotle the Philosopher*. Oxford: Oxford University Press, 1981.

Barnes, J., *Aristotle*. Oxford: Oxford University Press, 1982.

Grene, Marjorie. *A Portrait of Aristotle*. Chicago: University of Chicago Press, 1967.

Robinson, Timothy A. *Aristotle in Outline*. Indianapolis: Hackett Publishing Co., 1995.

Veatch, Henry B. *Aristotle: A Contemporary Appreciation*. Bloomington: Indiana University Press, 1974.

On Aristotle's political theory, see:

Jaffa, Harry. "Aristotle," in *History of Political Philosophy*, pp. 64–130. Second edition. Edited by Leo Strauss and Joseph Cropsey. Chicago: University of Chicago Press, 1981.

On the rediscovery and reception of Aristotle in the medieval world, see:

Steenberghen, Fernand van. *Aristotle in the West: The Origins of Latin Aristotelianism*. Translated by L. Johnson. New York: Humanities Press, 1970.

For an up-to-date, scholarly chronology of the life and works of Thomas Aquinas, see:

Torrell, Jean-Pierre. *St. Thomas Aquinas*. Volume I: *The Person and His Work*. Translated by Robert Royal. Washington, D.C.: The Catholic University of America Press, 1996.

Tugwell, Simon. "Introduction to St. Thomas," in *Albert and Thomas: Selected Writings*, pp. 201–351. New York: Paulist Press, 1988.

For an accurate and well-integrated English condensation of the *Summa*, see:

Aquinas, Thomas. *Summa Theologiae: A Concise Translation*. Edited and translated by Timothy McDermott. Westminster, Md.: Christian Classics, 1989.

For a guide to the context of Aquinas's thought, see:

Pieper, Joseph. *Guide to Thomas Aquinas*. Translated by Richard and Clara Winston. New York: Pantheon, 1962.

For expositions of Aquinas's general philosophy, see:

Copleston, Frederick. *A History of Philosophy.* Volume 2, pp. 302–424. Westminster, Md.: Newman, 1950. Also available in Image Books, Doubleday. Volume 2, part 2.

Davies, Brian. *The Thought of Thomas Aquinas.* Oxford: Oxford University Press, 1992.

Gilson, Etienne. *The Christian Philosophy of St. Thomas Aquinas.* New York: Random House, 1956.

McInerny, Ralph. *A First Glance at St. Thomas Aquinas: A Handbook for Peeping Thomists.* Notre Dame, Ind.: University of Notre Dame Press, 1990.

On Thomism and Aristotelianism, see:

Jaffa, Harry. *Thomism and Aristotelianism.* Chicago: University of Chicago Press, 1952.

On the ethics of Aquinas in general, see:

Aquinas, Thomas. *Commentary on the Ethics.* Translated by Charles I. Litzenger. Chicago: Regnery, 1963.

———. *Virtue: Way to Happiness* [selections from the Summa]. Translated by Richard J. Regan. Scranton: Scranton University Press, 1999.

Elders, Leon J., and Hedwig, K., editors. *The Ethics of St. Thomas Aquinas.* Studi tomistici 25. Vatican City: Libreria Editrice Vaticana, 1984.

———. *Lex et Libertas: Freedom and Law According to St. Thomas Aquinas.* Studi tomistici 30. Vatican City: Libreria Editrice Vaticana, 1987.

Mullady, Brian T. *The Meaning of the Term "Moral" in St. Thomas Aquinas.* Studi tomistici 27. Vatican City: Libreria Editrice Vaticana, 1986.

Stevens, G. "Moral Obligation in St. Thomas." *The Modern Schoolman,* 40 (1962–1963):1–21.

On choice and human action, see:

Donagan, Alan. *Human Ends and Human Action: An Exploration in St. Thomas's Treatment.* Milwaukee: Marquette University Press, 1985.

———. *Choice: The Essential Element in Human Action.* New York: Routledge, 1987.

Powell, Ralph. *Freely Chosen Reality.* Washington, D.C.: University Press of America, 1983.

Sokolowski, Robert. *Moral Action: A Phenomenological Study.* Bloomington: Indiana University Press, 1985.

On virtue, see:

Geach, Peter. *The Virtues.* Cambridge: Cambridge University Press, 1977.

Pieper, Joseph. *The Four Cardinal Virtues: Prudence, Fortitude, Justice, and Temperance.* New York: Harcourt, Brace, and World, 1965.

Porter, Mildred J. *The Recovery of Virtue: The Relevance of Aquinas for Christian Ethics.* Louisville: John Knox Press, 1990.

On practical wisdom, see:

Westberg, Daniel. *Right Practical Reason: Aristotle, Action, and Prudence in Aquinas.* Oxford: Oxford University Press, 1994.

On Thomist natural law, see:

Aquinas, Thomas. *A Treatise on Law.* ST I–II, QQ. 90–7. Translated, with commentary, by Robert J. Henle. Notre Dame, Ind.: University of Notre Dame Press, 1993.

Armstrong, Ross A. *Primary and Secondary Precepts in Thomistic Natural Law Teaching.* The Hague: Nijhoff, 1966.

Lee, Patrick. "Permanence of the Ten Commandments: St. Thomas and His Modern Commentators." *Theological Studies* 42 (1981):422–43.

May, William. *Becoming Human: An Introduction to Christian Ethics.* Dayton: Plaum, 1975.

Regan, Richard J. Chapter 1, "The Human Person and Moral Norms," in *The Moral Dimensions of Politics*, pp. 12–28. New York: Oxford University Press, 1986.

Reilly, James P. *St. Thomas on Law.* Etienne Gilson Series 12. Toronto: Pontifical Institute of Medieval Studies, 1990.

Rhonheimer, Martin. *Natural Law and Practical Reason: A Thomist View of Moral Autonomy.* Translated by Gerald Malsbary. New York: Fordham University Press, 1999.

Simon, Yves. *The Tradition of Natural Law: A Philosopher's Reflections.* New York: Fordham University Press, 1965.

On contemporary interpretations of natural law, see:

Finnis, John M. *Natural Law and Natural Rights.* Oxford: Clarendon Press, 1980.

———. *Fundamentals of Ethics.* Washington, D.C.: Georgetown University Press, 1983.

George, Robert P. *Natural Law Theory: Contemporary Essays.* Oxford: Oxford University Press, 1992.

Hittinger, Russell. *Critique of the New Natural Law Theory.* Notre Dame, Ind.: University of Notre Dame Press, 1987.

On Aquinas's political philosophy, see:

Aquinas, Thomas. "Commentary on the *Politics* of Aristotle" [selections], in *Medieval Political Philosophy*, pp. 298–334. Edited by Ralph Lerner and Muhsin Mahdi. Translated by Ernest L. Fortin and Peter D. O'Neill. New York: Free Press, 1963.

Bigongiari, Dino. "Introduction," *The Political Ideas of Saint Thomas Aquinas*, pp. vii–xxxvii. New York: Hafner, 1953.

Finnis, John M. *Aquinas: Moral, Political, and Legal Theory.* New York: Oxford University Press, 1999.

Fortin, Ernest L. "St. Thomas Aquinas," in *History of Political Philosophy*, pp. 223–50. Second edition. Edited by Leo Strauss and Joseph Cropsey. Chicago: University of Chicago Press, 1981.

Maritain, Jacques. *Man and the State.* Chicago: University of Chicago Press, 1951.

Regan, Richard J. "Aquinas on Political Obedience and Disobedience." *Thought* 56 (March 1981):77–88.

————. Chapter 2, "The Human Person and Organized Society: Aquinas," in *The Moral Dimensions of Politics*, pp. 37–46. New York: Oxford University Press, 1986.

For a Thomist philosophy of democracy, see:

Simon, Yves. *Philosophy of Democratic Government.* Chicago: University of Chicago Press, 1961.

On a recent bibliography of Aquinas, see:

Ingardia, Richard. *Thomas Aquinas: International Bibliography, 1977–1990.* Bowling Green, Oh.: Philosophical Documentation Center, Bowling Green State University, 1993.

INDEX

Ambrose, St., 72
Aristotle: on certitude, 53; on the
common good, 72; on distinction
of natural from positive law, 46,
47; on human beings as social
animals, 50; on judges, 44, 45, 46;
on judgment and knowledge, 24,
25; on justice in general, 87; on
knowledge of particular human
actions, 65; on law and custom, 65;
on law and fear of punishment, 79;
on law and political community, 3,
5; on law and virtue, 4, 5, 19, 21,
78; on laws commanding virtuous
acts, 55, 72–73; on legal
justice, 38, 45, 52; on the measure
of reason, 10; on measures, 10, 52,
53, 54, 63; on metaphorical
justice, 73; on natural justice, 38,
40, 46, 75, 76–77; on necessary
things, 28; on the need for forms
to be suitable for ends, 48; on
object of human law, 72–73; on
opinions of the prudent, 47; on
particularity and laws, 46, 52, 53;
on pleasure in virtuous habits, 80;
on properties of the soul, 33; on
reason, 28, 39; on regimes, 51, 72,
89; on right order and rulers, 88;
on tyrannical laws, 18; on understanding first principles, 35; on
virtue, 18, 31, 78, 79; on virtue of
rulers and subjects, 18, 19; on the
virtuous and good fortune, 90
Augustine, St.: on acting contrary to
the letter of the law, 60; on custom
as law, 66; on the error of
Pelagius, 80–81; on eternal law, 7,
8, 9, 22, 24, 30, 31; on evil, 19; on

habits, 33; on human law, 12, 25,
26, 54, 55; on kinds of law, 10; on
natural law, 43; on natures of
things, 22, 23; on the Old Law and
the Gospel, 14; on the Old Testament prefiguring Christ, 86; on
political community, 52; on
regimes, 64; on revision of
laws, 63; on truth, 24; on unjust
laws, 46, 57; on virtue and servile
fear, 20; on the Word, 23, 28

Basil, St., 33, 34
Boethius, 35

Caesar, Julius, 40
Cicero: on human law, 10, 46; on jus-
tice, 48
Conscience, 56–58
Concupiscence, 15–17, 25, 26
Custom and law, 65–67

Damascene, St. John: on sin, 38; on
virtue, 37
Decalogue: on dispensation
from, 75–78; and moral precepts
of Old Law, 73–75

Gratian (*Decretum*): on human laws,
4, 6, 58, 65; on natural law, 38, 40,
41
Gregory IX, Pope (*Decretals*), 60

Hilary, St., 63

Isidore, St.: on custom and law, 66;
on derivation of law, 6; on human
laws, 44, 48, 52, 53, 54, 66, 67; on
kinds of laws, 46, 49–50, 51; on